Learning

THE PROFESSIONAL EDUCATION FOR TEACHERS SERIES

Under the Editorship of PAUL WOODRING

Editor of the Educational Supplement of the Saturday Review
and Distinguished Service Professor at Western Washington State College

PUBLISHED TITLES

Introduction to American Education, Paul Woodring

Education and Democratic Ideals, Gordon C. Lee

Education in Western Culture, Robert Ulich

American Secondary Schools, Mauritz Johnson, Jr.

Teaching in a World of Change, Robert H. Anderson

Measuring Pupil Achievement and Aptitude, C. M. Lindvall

Learning, J. Charles Jones

Volumes on the following topics are in preparation: Social Psychology in Education, Human Growth and Development, Elementary Education.

Learning

J. CHARLES JONES

Bucknell University

Harcourt, Brace & World, Inc.
New York · Chicago · San Francisco · Atlanta

Library of Congress Catalog Card Number: 67-16824

Printed in the United States of America

Editor's Foreword

An understanding of the learning process is central to both the discipline of psychology and the profession of teaching. If teachers are to make the best possible use of the knowledge and understanding that psychologists have accumulated through more than sixty years of careful research, they must be aware both of the conclusions reached and of the nature of the evidence. But the published research on learning is so vast and complex that no beginning teacher can be expected to be familiar with more than a small portion of it. And the application of psychological knowledge to classroom practice is complicated by the fact that, in the words of William James, "Psychology is a science—teaching is an art; and sciences never generate arts directly out of themselves. An intermediate inventive mind must make the application, by use of its originality."

Teachers in training need a brief and readable but intellectually sophisticated interpretation of the research findings on learning, written by an educational psychologist who is thoroughly familiar with the research but who also understands the problems faced by teachers. This volume presents such an interpretation. Its purpose is to bring the science of psychology to bear on the art of teaching.

This book reflects Dr. Jones's many years of experience as an educational psychologist, his understanding of children and adolescents, and his scholarly knowledge of learning theory. The author knows the problems faced by teachers in their everyday contacts with children and has thought deeply about the psychological implications of those problems. He has selected his material with care and has presented it in clear language with appropriate illustrations of possible applications.

This volume, like others in the present series, may be used in any of a variety of ways. In colleges that offer a single comprehensive course in educational psychology, it may be used in conjunction with other books in the series, particularly those on child development, social psychology, and testing and evaluation. Where a separate course in learning is offered for teachers, this volume, rounded out by the readings listed at the end of each chapter, may be used as the basic text. However it is used, those students who read it and who discuss with their colleagues the questions found at the end of each chapter, will be better teachers as a result of the experience.

PAUL WOODRING

Preface

Most books written for teachers are guesses about the future—the future of our educational practices and the futures of the teachers who read the books. This book is a guess—but not a blind one, I hope—about the sorts of things teachers need to know about the psychology of learning.

Probably no two psychologists will make exactly the same guess, in part because they are likely to disagree over the validity and relative usefulness of some psychological theories, concepts, and data. And, in their roles as soothsayers, they will probably also differ over the tasks and problems they see teachers facing in the future.

The question, therefore, is really not "What do teachers need to know about learning?" Rather, it is "Of all the things that teachers might learn about the nature of learning, which will be most useful today—and a year, five years, or twenty years from today?"

While we must guess at the answer to this question, some guesses, it seems to me, are more reasonable than others. Presenting to teachers a series of prescriptions for dealing with problems of learning is one answer. But, whether or not this advice is based on psychological principles, it calls for certain assumptions that are difficult to justify. One must assume that the teachers' professional environment will remain relatively stable, with the same problems and instructional tasks arising repeatedly. And one must assume that he can anticipate all or most of these problems. This approach may be helpful temporarily, particularly to the beginning teacher, but in the long run it shortchanges him because it does not provide a basis for solving new and unanticipated problems. Nor is it particularly flattering to the teacher. Most teachers, certainly most *good* teachers, are capable of functioning above this craft level and are able to analyze their problems and their performances within a theoretical framework, provided they have such a framework.

On the other hand, while teachers can profit from a theoretical analysis of learning, I do not believe it essential or even very useful for them to spend their time considering the relative merits of various learning theories. What is offered here is a theoretical discussion of learning but not a discussion of learning theories. Some readers will note a definite bias in favor of S-R explanations, but this is not because I am convinced that this is the only theoretical model or even the best one to present to teachers. However, it does seem to be a useful way of thinking about learning, and there are some advantages in maintaining a consistent perspective.

Where possible, I have drawn upon research on human learning. In some cases, however, I have referred to research on animal behavior. With those who contend that "rats and monkeys aren't children," I can only agree. But an important point is being missed here: psychologists interested in learning are not studying rats, monkeys, or children. They are studying a phenomenon that occurs in each of these and in a great many other organisms, the phenomenon of learning.

This, then, is a book about learning—or a way of thinking about and studying learning. It has little or nothing to say directly and specifically about teaching procedures. But it is written in the hope that a clearer understanding of the nature of learning—together with intelligence and ingenuity—will lead to improved teaching.

I am indebted to the many psychologists upon whose research I have drawn, to my colleagues, and to those who have taught me, especially Marvin D. Glock and Frank S. Freeman of Cornell. I am also happy to express my appreciation to my wife, who listened patiently to the several revisions of the manuscript, and to Emily K. Foust, who as patiently typed them.

J. CHARLES JONES

Contents

Foreword v

Preface vii

Chapter One 3

Education and Behavioral Change

Psychology and the Study of Behavioral Change
The Teacher and the Learning Process
Characteristics of the Learner. Nature of the Material to Be Learned. Presentation Variables. Practice Variables. Reinforcement Variables. The Learning Environment. Theories of Instruction.
The Teacher and Learning Theory

Chapter Two 24

Characteristics of Learning

Respondent Behavior
Instrumental Behavior
Reinforcement
Secondary Reinforcement
Extinction and Spontaneous Recovery
Learning Characteristics and Teaching

Chapter Three 47

Motivation: Basic Concepts

Drive Approaches
Stimulus Approaches
Motivation: A Reconsideration

Chapter Four 63

Motivation and Learning

Motivation and Performance
Emotions as Motives
Punishment and Motivation
Social Motivation

Chapter Five 84

Verbal Behavior and Concept Formation

Language as an Intervening Variable
Language as Instrumental Behavior
The Acquisition of Meaning
Concept Formation
Concept-Formation Tasks. Language and Concept Formation. Teaching and Concept Formation.

Chapter Six 109

Retention

Problems in the Measurement of Retention
Theories of Forgetting
Variables Related to Retention
Nature of the Material. Reorganization and Recoding. The Total Stimulus Pattern. Degree of Learning. Intent.

Chapter Seven 126

Transfer

Theories of Transfer
Generalization and Discrimination in Transfer
Variables in Transfer
Predifferentiation. Organization and Level of Learning. Task Difficulty. Ability of the Learner.
The Nature of Transfer: A Reappraisal
Transfer and Teaching

Chapter Eight 147

Complex Behavior: Skills and Problem Solving

Skills

The Learning of Skill Performances. Demonstration and Guidance in the Acquisition of Skills. Practice and the Learning of Skills. Summary: The Importance of Skill Performance.

Problem Solving

Variables Affecting Problem-Solving Performance. Problem Solving in Groups.

Index 175

Learning

Chapter One

Education and Behavioral Change

The purpose of education is to change behavior. To those who think of education as a means of expanding the horizons of one's world, of understanding the past as well as preparing for the future, such a statement may seem hopelessly and pointlessly restricted. They may insist that, while certain behavioral changes are *among* the goals of education, the real purposes should be to acquire the values of one's culture, to develop literary and artistic appreciations, and to understand one's self and the world in which one lives. Others, taking a more immediate view, may maintain that they are not interested in changing behavior but that they want children to understand mathematics, to learn the rules of good grammar, and to think clearly and effectively.

Others may object to the view of education as an attempt to change behavior out of an aversion to the idea of controlling and manipulating the individual to meet the requirements of society. Our political and social traditions incline us to view education as a liberating force in our society rather than as a means of controlling the behavior of its members. But, as Linton has observed,[1] culture is a series of ready-made solutions to problems, and even the most democratic cultures try, through their systems of education, to teach their members culturally acceptable solutions. To the extent that a culture can influence the individual to choose certain solutions and to reject others, it has, of course, succeeded in exerting control over his behavior.

It is obvious that we are changing behavior when we teach children to conform to the ways of their culture—when we toilet-train them, require them to use table utensils properly, and gen-

1. Ralph Linton, *The Tree of Culture* (New York: Knopf, 1955), p. 34.

erally see that they learn the essentials of living with others. The acquisition of these skills and understandings shows itself in changed behavior.

Even if we take an extremely narrow view and consider the goal of education to be simply to learn those subjects and skills ordinarily taught in our schools, behavioral changes, while perhaps less apparent, remain the fundamental goal. The child who has learned to read behaves differently when he looks at a book from the child who has not learned to read. Ink marks on the page become stimuli of a different sort to him, and he responds to them differently. A major source of stimulation is opened up to him, multiplying and extending his ability to learn and resulting in additional behavioral changes. Through reading, he encounters new ideas, acquires information previously inaccessible to him, and, perhaps, learns new skills. There may be other concomitant behavioral changes. He may stay up late reading, dawdle over a book while dressing, or read every word on the cereal box even though the school bus is due.

PSYCHOLOGY AND THE STUDY OF BEHAVIORAL CHANGE

The task of the scientist is to test statements about the world of events. The particular events in which the psychologist is interested are *behavioral* events, and he, like any other scientist, attempts to determine whether or not there are regularities in these events. Some behavioral events—the actions, words, judgments, and choices of individuals—he can observe directly. Sensations, emotional attachments, perceptions, needs, and images, on the other hand, while "psychological," are not susceptible to direct scientific observation. Psychology is not the only area in which certain phenomena are impalpable; no one has ever seen magnetism, heat, or gravity any more than anyone has ever seen a motive. This does not mean that such phenomena cannot be studied objectively and scientifically; it does mean that knowledge of them must come from observable events—events whose occurrence can be agreed upon by more than one observer. We must be able to observe the deflection of a needle on a dial or a change in an individual's responses, and we must be able to agree on whether or not these events actually do occur. It is for this reason that the psychologist redefines in terms of observable behaviors such educational objectives as "improving children's ability to think" or "changing students' goals." His purpose is not to question the validity of the educator's objectives. If the psychologist is to help the educator, he must be able to study by methods of psychology the steps by which these objectives are attained.

Marston Bates has written of the problem of the biologist who, after being asked to identify some animal, is almost inevitably asked another question: "What good is it?" Bates comments, "I have never learned how to deal with this question. I am left appalled by the point of view that makes it possible. I don't know where to start explaining the world of nature that the biologist sees, in which 'What good is it?' becomes meaningless." [2]

Yet, to the farmer whose experience leads him to consider animals from the viewpoint of their effects upon crops and to the suburban householder who is worried about his roses, this may seem an eminently reasonable question, and they may be annoyed or confused by the biologist's failure to answer it simply and directly. In much the same way, the parent or the teacher may find the dimensions of the psychologist's world of behavioral events unfamiliar. To the psychologist they may seem to be asking all the wrong questions, and to them he may be failing to give reasonable answers.

Bates does, in fact, present a lucid view of the world as the biologist perceives it, and what the biologist has to say about his world can be not only interesting but tremendously important to those of us who are not biologists. If the work of the behavioral scientist is to be of similar importance to parents and educators, his viewpoint must also be understood. If it is not, misunderstandings and estrangements will continue to occur. The educator will not receive the assistance he needs, and many of the questions that intrigue the psychologist will go unanswered.

To be sure, the psychologist's is not the only possible view of the purpose of education. We may feel that man has a special and distinct nature and existence and that the empirical, quantitative approach of the behavioral scientist, which may be successful in studying simpler forms of life, cannot give us anything like a complete knowledge of man. It is apparent that the mechanistic explanations of the psychologist are not completely adequate for an

---

2. Marston Bates, *The Forest and the Sea* (New York: Mentor, 1960), p. 10.

understanding of our fellow man or for control over ourselves. Nevertheless, much of man's behavior and man's society can be studied productively from a mechanistic viewpoint. The approach of the behavioral scientist, though limited, is not necessarily invalid because of its limitations, and most of the progress we have made in understanding and predicting man's behavior has come through this approach.

The psychologist sometimes finds himself caught between opposing types of criticism. One of his major concerns is to predict behavior—that is, to determine the antecedent conditions that appear to influence or produce a particular piece of behavior. Quite obviously the ability to specify these conditions precisely and completely could give control over the behavior itself. Consequently, the intentions of the psychologist are sometimes questioned, and he may be accused of attempting to manipulate the behavior of his fellow men, invading their privacy and seeking to control society. At the same time, he is criticized for failing to provide direct and immediate assistance to parents, teachers, and others who wish to change and control human behavior.

What, then, are the limitations of psychology? What, in fact, can educators legitimately expect from it?

Some of the limitations of psychology arise from its very nature. Since psychology deals only with *behavioral events* whose occurrence can be agreed upon by more than a single individual, it cannot answer questions about the truth or reality of subjective individual experiences. The psychologist may be able to predict the consequences of punishing a child for lying, but he cannot provide a scientific answer to the question of whether it is moral to punish him. Psychology, therefore, while it can deal with the behavioral consequences of procedures aimed at changing and controlling behavior, cannot answer the question of whether society *should* follow such procedures.

Other limitations of psychology arise from the complexity of its subject matter. Gilbert Highet's description of the human brain, while literary rather than scientific, suggests some of the complexities with which the psychologist tries to deal:

> Day and night, from childhood to old age, sick or well, asleep or awake, men and women think. The human brain works like the heart, ceaselessly pulsing. In its three pounds weight of tissue are recorded and stored billions upon billions of memories, habits, in-

stincts, abilities, desires, hopes, fears, patterns and tinctures and sounds and inconceivably delicate calculations and brutishly crude urgencies, the sound of a whisper heard thirty years ago, the resolution impressed by daily practice for fifteen thousand days, the hatred cherished since childhood, the delight never experienced but incessantly imagined, the complex structure of the stresses in a bridge, the exact pressure of a single finger on a single string, the development of ten thousand different games of chess, the precise curve of a lip, a hill, an equation or a flying ball, tones and shades and glooms and raptures, the faces of countless strangers, the scent of one garden, prayers, inventions, crimes, poems, jokes, tunes, sums, problems unsolved, victories long past, the fear of Hell and the love of God, the vision of a blade of grass and the vision of the sky filled with stars.[3]

To study the complicated world of human behavior the psychologist makes careful observations and then draws inferences from those observations. And to keep his observations as accurate and as uncontaminated as possible he tries to isolate and control any variables that may affect them. In this he does not differ from other scientists. But the subject matter of the psychologist studying human behavior is vastly more complex than the materials studied by the physicist or the biochemist, and the factors that complicate his observations are correspondingly more difficult to control.

Consider, for example, the difficulties of the psychologist who wishes to study the effects of distracting stimuli on human learning. There are some obvious variables he must consider: the learning capacity of the subjects; their previous experience with the material to be learned; their experience working under distracting conditions; their ages; whether they are fatigued or rested; the types of distracting stimulus employed; and individual differences in sensitivity to this stimulation. But there are other, less obvious factors that may affect the outcome of the experiment—factors that are less accessible and more difficult to measure or control. Subjects may bring to the experiment attitudes about the material they are to learn, about psychologists, or about psychological experiments that may have a critical effect on the results or, at the very least, limit the applicability of the results in nonexperimental situations. Even the subjects' comprehension of the purpose of an experiment may affect their behavior. One experimenter, engaged in a conditioning experiment using electric shock, found one of his student

3. Gilbert Highet, *Man's Unconquerable Mind* (New York: Columbia University Press, 1954), pp. 119–20.

subjects withstanding searing voltages without observable response because he thought the purpose of the experiment was "to see how much guts I had."

A further limitation of psychology is a lack of principles applicable to a wide range of behaviors. Psychology is a comparative newcomer among the sciences. Neither its subject matter nor its methodology have been completely defined, and psychologists have tried many different approaches. Because of the complex nature of behavior, however, most individual psychologists have chosen to restrict their investigations to a few relatively narrow problems. One result has been a lack of the unifying principles available to scientists in other disciplines.

THE TEACHER AND THE LEARNING PROCESS

If we accept the psychologists' view of education as a process of changing behavior, what can psychology tell us about these behavioral changes? Despite its limitations, does psychology have anything useful to say to the teacher about learning? In answering these questions, it is helpful first to consider two other questions: What are the teacher's fundamental concerns about learning? What are the major learning variables with which teachers must deal?

These are two different questions, though they are often confused. An examination of them may give us some understanding of how the teacher's view of learning diverges from that of the psychologist. Moreover, these questions provide a frame of reference for considering the relationship of psychology, and particularly of human learning, to the instructional activities of teachers.

The principal concerns of the teacher about learning are these: What is being learned, and how accurately is it being learned? How rapidly is learning taking place? How well is the learned material being retained? Will this learning transfer—that is, will the student be able to apply it in other circumstances, and will it help or hinder subsequent learning?

A tremendous and bewildering array of variables may influence the course of learning. Even the experienced teacher may conclude that human learning is so complicated that an analysis of the teaching-learning process is hopelessly beyond our ability to consider in any systematic manner. Some of the confusion may be reduced, however, if we consider the *major groups of variables* that affect learning.

Characteristics of the Learner. Theories of learning and educational practices would both be greatly simplified if it could be demonstrated that all learning reduces to certain fundamental elements. The attempts of psychologists to determine if this is actually the case have been complicated by the fact that individuals differ greatly in their learning potential and in their readiness or predisposition to learn. These differences arise from variations in intelligence and motivation, the effects of previous experiences that facilitate or inhibit learning, the physical state of the learner, and the task the learner sets himself—that is, what he is trying to do, which often differs from what the teacher thinks he is trying to do or wants him to do. These differences interact with one another in affecting learning, and our knowledge of the complex role each plays is imperfect. Intelligence, at least intelligence as measured by intelligence tests, is unquestionably affected by experience and by motivational factors. But the kinds of experience an individual has are also frequently a function of his intelligence or his motivation.

Nature of the Material to Be Learned. Whether or not the same basic principles of learning apply in discovering how to factor a polynomial, learning to tie a bow tie, and developing a tolerance for the behavior of one's roommate, we recognize that the tasks are different and that we set about learning each of them in a somewhat different manner.

What makes one learning task different from or more difficult than another? Some psychologists have classified learning tasks as *cognitive*—the acquisition of knowledge through perception, judgment, and reason; *affective*—learning pertaining to attitudes, feelings, or emotion; or *psychomotor*—the learning of manipulative skills. But other psychologists contend that these categories do not reflect fundamental differences in the underlying learning process. Even within a given category, some tasks are more difficult to learn than others.

Some learning-task differences arise from variations in the meaningfulness of the material being learned. There is, for example, no very good reason that amber, rather than some other color, should mean "caution" or that the letter *b* should follow *a* in our alphabet. Such simple associations are arbitrary and must be learned on a rote basis. On the other hand, some responses can be logically related to associations that have already been acquired.

A student who knows the meaning of "cascade" will probably have little difficulty in learning the meaning of the Italian verb "*cascare.*"

Other differences in learning tasks result from variations in response similarity or stimulus similarity. Generally, it is easier to learn a new response that is similar to a response that has already been acquired than to learn an entirely new response. However, if the learner's task is to discriminate between two stimuli that are very similar, he may encounter difficulty. Young children may confuse the letters *d* and *b* and yet have little trouble distinguishing between *a* and *f*. Other task differences result from the number of stimuli with which the learner must deal and the number of responses he must learn. It is obviously more difficult to learn the entire alphabet than to learn only the first three letters.

Presentation Variables. Most teachers believe that the manner in which material is presented to the learner can have a critical effect upon learning; and research supports this view. But critics point out that teachers tend to organize learning tasks in ways that are logical to teachers but that may not be the best ways of arranging and presenting materials to students who lack the teachers' experience.

Bruner has suggested how knowledge might be structured so that it is most readily grasped by the learner.[4] Optimal structuring of knowledge, according to Bruner, requires that we consider three characteristics of the material to be learned: (1) the manner in which a particular area of knowledge is represented through symbolic propositions, actions, procedures, or images (*mode of representation*); (2) the number of separate items of information that must be carried and processed by the learner in order for him to understand something (*economy*); and (3) the capacity of a particular structuring of knowledge to lead to solutions, to generate new propositions, and to increase the manipulability of a body of knowledge (*effective power*).

Educators have commonly assumed that certain subjects are to be taught at a certain grade level because they have an innate

4. Jerome S. Bruner, "Some Theorems on Instruction Illustrated with Reference to Mathematics," in E. Hilgard, ed., *Theories of Learning and Instruction,* Sixty-Third Yearbook of the National Society for the Study of Education, Part I (Chicago: University of Chicago Press, 1964), pp. 309–13.

level of difficulty that makes them appropriate to the learning ability of most students in that grade. However, as Bruner points out, we can change the terminology, symbols, or actions by which we represent some area of knowledge; we can change the number of pieces of information the learner must acquire; and we can organize knowledge in ways that affect its future usefulness.

We can, for example, present the concept of division and the operation of dividing to children in a number of ways. We can vary our mode of representation; we can use mathematical symbols, verbal explanations, graphic representations, or three-dimensional objects that can be divided into parts. The actual process of division can be taught by rote or by explaining the principles of division and the relationship of division to addition and multiplication. The first procedure requires the child to retain, in proper sequence, many more pieces of information; in Bruner's sense of the word, it lacks "economy." From the standpoint of the child's future ability to solve new problems and generate new mathematical insights, this step-by-step method is probably inferior to instruction requiring the learning of principles; in Bruner's terms, it lacks "effective power."

Many people, including some teachers, see the teacher as essentially a dispenser of information—in effect, an animated textbook. Teachers do, of course, provide the learner with information, but they also carry on other important activities in the teaching-learning process. We hope that students, by imitating the performance of teachers, will write more neatly, pronounce foreign words more accurately, and construct sentences more grammatically. Teachers also provide the learner with *guidance* by piloting him through the process or activity he is trying to learn—placing his fingers in the correct position, correcting the manner in which he holds a pencil, or demonstrating to him how to place his tongue in order to pronounce a certain sound.

Practice Variables. No matter how effectively teachers organize and present material, many of the things we expect students to master cannot be learned in a single trial. Many children, for example, spend years learning to read and write efficiently. Even such relatively simple tasks as tying a shoe or buttoning a shirt require practice.

There is a considerable body of folklore about the effects of various practice procedures on learning. Teachers and, through them, students are told that short practice periods with alternating rest periods are superior to massed practice, that practicing by wholes is preferable to breaking a task down into parts, that "active" practice is preferable to passive. It is often stated in texts written for teachers that when we are trying to learn a psychomotor skill we should strive first for accuracy and concern ourselves with speed only after accuracy has been achieved.

Although there is considerable evidence to support all these statements, they are valid only under severely restricted conditions. Close study suggests that in some cases the results are due not so much to the practice method as to some less apparent variable. Recitation and other "active" practice procedures, for example, may owe their results primarily to the feedback they provide the learner. They enable him to judge and correct his performance, and they furnish him with an incentive by providing him with knowledge of successes and failures. Research in the learning of skills has also shown that some tasks change markedly when performance is speeded up, calling for some new responses to be learned rather than simply for old responses to be performed more rapidly.

Reinforcement Variables. It seems doubtful whether the use of programed materials will produce the educational revolution predicted by their more enthusiastic proponents. Programed materials have, however, had one important effect upon our schools: many teachers with little knowledge of learning theory have been made aware of the important role of immediate reinforcement in learning. Some advocates of programed instruction contend that the most serious shortcoming of conventional instruction is the lack of provision for systematic, positive reinforcement.[5]

The teacher who recognizes the importance of reinforcement and attempts to influence learning through reinforcement is confronted with two questions: What stimuli will serve as practical and effective reinforcers? What are the most effective ways of arranging for the application of reinforcements?

Whether a given stimulus will reinforce a response depends on the particular needs the learner is attempting to satisfy. But needs

---

5. B. F. Skinner, "Why Teachers Fail," *Saturday Review* (October 16, 1965), p. 80.

cannot be observed directly, and many stimuli have acquired, as a result of the learner's previous experiences, the capacity to reinforce certain of his responses. Money and grades, for example, are not innately reinforcing; they do not directly satisfy any need. But, as a result of our experiences with them, they can come to serve as potent reinforcers for a wide variety of behaviors.

Teachers attempting to select the most effective reinforcement are faced, therefore, with the twin difficulties of knowing neither the learner's needs at any given moment nor the nature of his previous experiences with potential reinforcers. As a result, they tend to rely heavily on three forms of reinforcement to which most human beings respond rather consistently: (1) knowledge of results, (2) praise or approval, and (3) the reduction of anxiety.

The effectiveness of programed instruction when well-constructed materials are used indicates that knowledge of results, provided it comes shortly after the response, can be an effective reinforcer for human learners. Adult approval, too, is probably an effective reinforcement for most children. By threatening to withdraw approval, by the use of tests, and in many other ways, teachers arouse students' anxieties, thereby making it possible to use anxiety reduction as a reinforcer of desired behavior. Each of us knows the feeling of relief that accompanies passing an examination or successfully answering a question before the class.

However, probably as a result of unfortunate experiences with adults, some children may not regard adults as consistent or worthwhile sources of approval. There is also some evidence that grades and other signs of adult approval are more effective with middle-class children than with those from lower socioeconomic classes. Moreover, as a student matures there may be changes in his response to adult approval. James Coleman has suggested that during adolescence the really important source of approval for students is their own adolescent society.[6]

While teachers have been concerned with the question of the most effective kind of reinforcement, psychologists have also been interested in two other reinforcement variables: the effects of different schedules of reinforcement and the consequences of varying the interval between response and reinforcement. On the basis of their research, they have been able to suggest a number of ways in

---

6. James S. Coleman, *The Adolescent Society* (New York: Free Press of Glencoe, 1961), pp. 50–51.

which these variables might be manipulated. Unfortunately, teachers are often instructing twenty or thirty students at the same time, a state of affairs that makes it virtually impossible to reinforce each learner promptly and on any systematic schedule. B. F. Skinner has stated that the kinds of contingencies of reinforcement necessary for efficient learning are rarely present in the typical classroom.[7]

The Learning Environment. We go to considerable pains to provide well-ventilated classrooms with good lighting and cheerful color schemes, and yet we know very little about the effect of the physical environment upon learning. Pleasant, attractive surroundings may be justified on humanitarian and esthetic grounds, and they may even be of some indirect value in attracting the learner and keeping him in the learning situation. But, when we exclude materials and equipment directly related to instruction, it seems that people learn about as well in one type of environment as in another. This may be attributable to the learner's ability to focus his attention on the immediate learning situation and to the ability of human beings to "adapt out" most reasonably constant and not actually harmful stimulation. When we are concentrating upon some task, we are often oblivious of our physical environment.

Although the physical environment appears to be relatively unimportant in its effects upon learning, the *social* aspects of the learner's environment—that is, those aspects consisting of other human beings, including teachers—appear to exert a great deal of influence upon him, particularly with regard to *what* he learns. Studies of group influences suggest the power of such influences in controlling behavior, including learning behavior, and also indicate that the teacher's part in determining what is learned may often be less important than we care to acknowledge. It is apparently possible that both the physical and the social environment may become part of the total stimulus pattern affecting the learner, with subsequent effects upon his ability to transfer what he has learned to other situations. Memorizing a speech in one's room may, for this reason, be poor preparation for giving the same speech in a crowded auditorium.

---

7. B. F. Skinner, "Why We Need Teaching Machines," *Harvard Educational Review* (Fall 1961), pp. 377–98.

The above set of variables represents one way of analyzing the task of the teacher. It would be misleading, however, to suggest that the teacher can deal with these variables one at a time, that they operate independently of one another, or that changes in one leave the others unaffected. In many learning situations the nature of the material to be learned may affect both the mode of presentation and the type of practice procedures. Memorization by rote, for example, may be an effective technique for learning the alphabet, but it is not the best technique for learning mathematical principles or for acquiring an understanding of the concept of democracy. The manner in which the teacher attempts to structure the material to be learned is often partly determined by the maturity, intelligence, and experience of the learner.

Theories of Instruction. Teachers and psychologists find no difficulty in agreeing that the variables we have considered have a major influence on learning. However, their interests in these variables tend to follow divergent paths.

The teacher is likely to be concerned with whether or not a particular manipulation of variables results in more efficient learning, improved retention, or greater transfer. The psychologist is, of course, interested in these questions, too; but he is likely to be interested in explaining the results within some theoretical framework.

If a teacher is interested in theory, he is usually interested in a *theory of instruction* rather than a *theory of learning*. For this reason, teachers are often disappointed and disillusioned by their study of psychology. The psychologist, they find, views the study of human learning as just that: *the study of how human beings learn*. He does not view it as the study of how teachers teach or what they should try to teach. As Gage has pointed out,[8] there is a basic distinction between theories of learning that interest psychologists and theories of instruction that interest teachers: theories of learning deal with the ways in which an organism learns; theories of instruction deal with the ways in which a person influences an organism to learn.

Logically, a theory of instruction should be concerned with two major topics: the manner in which the material to be learned

8. N. L. Gage, "Theories of Teaching," in Hilgard, *op. cit.*, p. 268.

should be arranged for presentation to the learner and the ways in which the teacher can facilitate the learning of this material. The study of human learning, teachers find, does not present them with information on these two subjects. They frequently see no immediate or direct applicability of learning theory to the problems they encounter in helping students learn. Neither do they find much help with the problem of selecting the sequences in which experiences would be best arranged for the most efficient learning.

That learning theory does not provide teachers directly with information on *how* to teach has been pointed out repeatedly by both educators and psychologists. Less attention has been given to the fact that learning theory has also had very little influence upon curriculum planning—upon the problems of *what* to teach. Curriculum construction has most frequently been concerned with the question of what subjects should be covered at given grade levels and with the logical arrangement of material within instructional units. Unfortunately, an arrangement that seems logical to a teacher who has already learned the material may not be the best arrangement for an inexperienced learner. It has been the rare textbook or course that has concerned itself with an analysis of curriculum organization based upon any consistent theory of how human beings learn.[9]

Recently, there have been indications that the gulf between theories of learning and theories of instruction may be narrowing. Some of the more recent textbooks on curriculum have attempted to consider the role of learning theory in curriculum organization. Jerome Bruner has suggested that a theory of instruction not only is a necessity if we are to test propositions about the best way to teach but is essential to developing an adequate theory of human learning.[10] Without such a theory, Bruner contends, we are likely to accept some *particular* description of learning as a description of *optimal* learning.

For Bruner, a theory of instruction would be concerned first with the question of the kinds of prior experience that are most likely to predispose the learner to learn. Second, it would be concerned

9. Glenn M. Blair, "How Learning Theory Is Related to Curriculum Organization," *Journal of Educational Psychology* (March 1948), pp. 161–66.
10. Bruner, *op. cit.*

with the way in which learners organize knowledge and with the best way in which to structure knowledge for the most effective learning. Finally, it would include a consideration of the sequence of encounters with the materials to be learned that is most likely to result in efficient learning. Bruner's approach provides only the barest framework of a theory of instruction, but it does represent a starting point, and it calls attention to the fact that what is needed is an explanation not simply of how learners learn but of how they learn under the most favorable circumstances.

Since instruction is the central concern of teachers, they understandably tend to view learning in terms of such externals as the curriculum or the learning environment, including the teacher and his activities. The teacher and the nature of the material to be learned certainly are important variables in learning. But we must remind ourselves that learning not only *can,* but very frequently *does,* take place in the absence of a teacher or of organized learning material. This is not to say that teachers play no part in the learning process, that unassisted learning does not sometimes result in the learning of some things that perhaps should never be learned, or that greater efficiency is not possible through an organized instruction program. But our concern over teachers and curricula may lead us to overlook the fact that learning is something that goes on within the learner; it is not something that is done to him by a teacher. Unfortunately for teachers, this is a common misapprehension of parents, students, and members of the general public, all of whom are inclined to view learning failures as synonymous with teaching failures. Teaching is but one of a number of variables affecting learning.

THE TEACHER AND LEARNING THEORY

Some educators maintain that learning theory is the concern of the psychologist, not the teacher, and that the teacher can play no real role in the development of theory, being at best a technician who applies theory and furnishes data. These educators acknowledge, however, that the teacher, without being directly concerned with learning theory, can derive some practical benefits from theories developed by others. Perhaps a more common position among educators is that learning theory is unnecessary and irrelevant to effective teaching. Those who take this position sometimes suggest that psychologists would be better occupied developing specific procedures applicable to the classroom.

Psychologists are not unaware of the ambiguous role that learning theory plays in education. They are generally agreed that learning theory does not directly suggest effective teaching procedures. Moreover, as Robert A. Davis has pointed out,[11] applications of psychological theories to educational practices, when they have been made, have sometimes been merely an attempt to provide a theoretical justification for some procedure that has already been decided upon. But do these criticisms and obvious gaps between learning theory and educational practices mean that theory is of no real utility to teachers?

It is true that some psychologists are unable to translate their knowledge of learning theory into effective teaching behavior. It is also true that some teachers are highly effective although they lack any theoretical knowledge of the learning process. These are individuals whose awareness and insight enable them to benefit to an unusual degree from their own experiences as teachers, and they are apparently able to retain and apply the results of these experiences in the classroom. But they are the exceptions. In teaching, as in many other areas, a rapidly growing body of knowledge is accompanying increasingly complex problems. The majority of us are simply taxed beyond our limits if we are required to remember empirically derived solutions to all conceivable problems that may confront us.

If ever any subject has *demanded* a theoretical approach, it is learning. Learning is something that goes on all about us and within us; we are all familiar with it. Yet, as Mowrer points out,[12] while psychologists refer to sensation, to perception, and to motivation, they customarily speak of learning *theory.* Sensations, perceptions, and desires are things we experience directly, but we do not have a comparable experience of learning while it is taking place. Notice your own behavior when you have learned something. The usual, immediate, verbal response is "Now I see," or "Now I can do it," or even "Now I understand," and only

11. Robert A. Davis, "Applicability of Applications of Psychology with Particular Reference to Schoolroom Learning," *Journal of Educational Research* (September 1943), pp. 19–30.
12. O. H. Mowrer, *Learning Theory and Behavior* (New York: Wiley, 1960), p. 13.

rarely "Now I am learning." Learning takes place without our being immediately aware of it. We recognize its operation only after the fact, because then we perceive some aspect of our environment differently or feel different about it or can do something that we could not do before. In attempting to understand learning, we are attempting to understand a process that is not directly accessible to our observations.

Some educators have maintained that teachers need theoretically derived *procedures,* rather than theoretically derived *explanations.* Such a viewpoint is understandable, but it indicates a failure to recognize the relationship of theory to application or of science to technology. Hilgard has pointed out that there may be as many as half a dozen steps from pure research on learning to the development of an instructional technology and its application in the classroom.[13] (See Figure 1.)

But, regardless of their expressed attitudes toward learning theory, teachers *do* operate on the basis of theories. The question is whether the theories are explicit and have been carefully considered by the teacher or whether they are implicit and unexamined. The teacher who contends, for example, that children can learn only if they are quiet and orderly has a theory about learning that will probably affect much of his classroom behavior. This theory—that learning is a by-product of order, control, and discipline—is not a very good theory, and the teacher has perhaps never really considered it as such, but it is a theory of learning nevertheless. One purpose of acquainting teachers with learning theory is to sensitize them to the fact that much of their teaching behavior may be based on such subterranean beliefs.

In considering the potential contribution of psychology to teaching, we should not overlook the fact that teachers can make a real contribution to psychology. The two groups—teachers and psychologists—are in a position to complement one another's activities. Psychologists are sometimes accused of engaging in highly specialized, if not trivial, research on very narrow aspects of behavior and of being remote from the classroom and from the real problems of both teachers and learners. Teachers, on the other hand, have been criticized for being oblivious to the subtleties of

13. E. Hilgard, "A Perspective on the Relationship between Learning Theory and Educational Practices," in Hilgard, *op. cit.,* pp. 402–15.

FIGURE 1

STEPS IN RESEARCH ON LEARNING—PURE RESEARCH TO TECHNICAL DEVELOPMENT

PURE RESEARCH			TECHNOLOGICAL RESEARCH AND DEVELOPMENT		
Not Directly Relevant	Relevant Subjects and/or Topics	School-relevant Subjects and Topics	Laboratory, Classroom, and Special Teacher	Tryout in "Normal" Classroom	Advocacy and Adoption
Step 1	*Step 2*	*Step 3*	*Step 4*	*Step 5*	*Step 6*
Animal mazes, eyelid conditioning, pursuit learning, etc.	Human verbal learning, concept formation, etc.	Mathematics, reading, typing, etc.	Programed instruction: language laboratory, in early stages	Results of Step 4 tried in regular setting	Manuals and textbooks prepared; teacher training undertaken

SOURCE: E. Hilgard, "A Perspective on the Relationship between Learning Theory and Educational Practices," in E. Hilgard, ed., *Theories of Learning and Instruction* (Chicago: University of Chicago Press, 1964).

human learning, for overgeneralizing from limited personal experience, and for ignoring theoretical approaches to an understanding of learning in favor of rule-of-thumb teaching procedures.

Although much teaching—perhaps most teaching—is based on individual experience rather than on any theoretical analysis of the teaching-learning process, teachers are capable of viewing teaching as a "profession" in the sense in which Whitehead used this term: as "an avocation whose activities are subjected to theoretical analysis and are modified by theoretical conclusions derived from that analysis." [14] And teachers are capable of approaching the study of human learning scientifically.

Scientific inquiry begins with observation—and with the questions and problems that observations raise. Teachers have unequaled opportunities for observing the learning behavior of children and adolescents. Provided they possess both a spirit of inquiry and some conceptual framework for guiding and organizing their observations, they could open imaginative, productive lines of inquiry. The infusion of a fresh viewpoint into the study of human learning could result in important new insights. It could lead to knowledge bearing directly upon classroom problems. We might discover really effective techniques for teaching culturally deprived children or more valid ways of assessing creativity. Or the outcome could be broader principles that would increase the ability of teachers to interpret their observations and translate them into improved theories of instruction.

Suggestions for Class Discussion and Further Investigation

1. What do you think you should learn from the study of human learning? Do you think this would be of more help to you in answering questions about education or in improving your ability to teach?
2. What are some important problems in education that do not fall within the field of human learning or educational psychology?
3. Frequently, after a discussion with teachers or parents, psychologists are asked, "When a child does such and such, what should I do?" The usual reply is, "I don't know. It all depends." Depends upon what?

---

14. A. N. Whitehead, *Adventures of Ideas* (New York: Macmillan, 1933), p. 72.

4. Consider some of the outstanding aspects of your own personality, including some that give you satisfaction and others that bother you. In the development of these characteristics, how influential was the school? What additional knowledge and skills might your teachers have needed to help you develop those favorable characteristics and eliminate those that were unfavorable?
5. Some teachers with little formal knowledge of psychology are remarkably effective in the classroom. Why not simply analyze the classroom behavior of these teachers and teach other teachers to behave in the same manner?

Suggestions for Further Reading

Contrasting viewpoints on the role of psychology in the prediction and control of human behavior are presented in Carl R. Rogers, "The Place of the Person in the New World of the Behavioral Sciences," *Personnel and Guidance Journal* (February 1961), and B. F. Skinner, *Walden II* (New York: Macmillan, 1948).

The relationship of research and psychology to education is discussed in the following articles in E. Hilgard, ed., *Theories of Learning and Instruction,* Sixty-Third Yearbook of the National Society for the Study of Education, Part I (Chicago: University of Chicago Press, 1964):

Frederick J. McDonald, "The Influence of Learning Theories on Education," pp. 1–26.

Robert Glaser, "Implications of Training Research for Education," pp. 153–81.

N. L. Gage, "Theories of Teaching," pp. 268–85.

Jerome S. Bruner, "Some Theorems on Instruction Illustrated with Reference to Mathematics," pp. 306–35.

A. A. Lumsdaine, "Educational Technology, Programed Learning, and Instructional Science," pp. 371–401.

E. Hilgard, "A Perspective on the Relationship between Learning Theory and Educational Practices"; and "Postscript: Twenty Years of Learning Theory in Relation to Education," pp. 402–18.

N. L. Gage, ed., *Handbook of Research on Teaching* (Chicago: Rand McNally, 1963), provides a comprehensive discussion of research methods and the results of research applicable to teaching.

The major theories of learning are presented in a condensed form in Winfred Hill, *Learning: A Survey of Psychological Interpretations* (San Francisco: Chandler, 1963). This book has been oriented toward educators, and the author attempts to point out educational applications of learning theory.

The assumptions made by adults about the nature of learning and the effects of these assumptions upon child-rearing practices are examined in Jane Loevinger, "Patterns of Parenthood as Theories of Learning," *Journal of Abnormal and Social Psychology* (July 1959), pp. 148–50.

Chapter Two

Characteristics of Learning

Not all human behavior is the result of learning. If we touch a hot object, we withdraw our hand hastily. Food in the mouth produces the response of salivation. These are unlearned responses. But under some circumstances we find that these responses are elicited by an entirely different set of stimuli. A sharply spoken "Hot!" produces a quick withdrawal of our hand, though there is nothing painful or dangerous about the command itself. When hungry we tend to salivate at the sight of the words "broiled steak." These are examples of learned behavior—that is, they are changes in behavior that result from experience, where one stimulus has become a substitute for another. We make the same responses of withdrawal and salivation, but now we respond to a sound (the spoken word "hot") and to a visual stimulus (printed words).

There is also another kind of behavioral change related to experience. The responses of young children to the things they want, for example, are usually simple and direct. They seize food and push it into their mouths; they snatch toys away from other children. As they gain experience, frequently with parents and older, stronger children, their behavior changes. The same stimuli come to produce new responses: food is eaten with knives and forks, and toys are traded rather than snatched.

Learning, then, seems to include changes of two different types. In some cases, a response previously made to one stimulus is now made to a different stimulus; in other instances, the old stimulus now elicits a different response. These deceptively simple changes have implications of major importance for the teacher and the psychologist, since, to the extent that a response can be shifted from one stimulus to another, behavior can be modified.

Are descriptions of these processes of stimulus substitution and response substitution descriptions of all learning? Is learning to read simply a more complex case of the same process that results in salivation at the sound of a bell? Since learning to ride a bicycle, learning to appreciate a Bach fugue, and learning to respond appropriately to the symbols in a mathematical problem all represent behavioral changes resulting from experience, each qualifies as an example of learning. Can they all be reduced to the same elements, or do they represent fundamentally different kinds of learning? These are questions that psychologists have debated for many years.

Learning is an explanation of certain changes in behavior; it is a hypothetical construct, not something that can be observed directly. Behavioral changes that are related to experience rather than to fatigue, physical change, deterioration, or the effects of chemicals, we explain as being the result of learning. At the moment, we are in no position to make conclusive statements about the internal mechanisms of learning—whether they are, for example, neurophysiological or biochemical in nature or whether there are fundamentally different kinds of learning. In psychology, as in other sciences, theories, explanations, and classification systems are almost inevitably based on incomplete information. Yet they can be useful when they fit the available data, help us make predictions, and do not obscure the possibility of other explanations. On the basis of differences in observable characteristics, we can consider learning under two categories. These differences include the nature of the changed behavior and the circumstances under which changes in behavior occur.

RESPONDENT BEHAVIOR

It seems reasonable to assume that children do not come into the world dreading arithmetic or that the pupils of college students' eyes do not ordinarily contract at the sound of a tone. Let us assume, however, that a child's initial experiences with arithmetic result in a series of failures, accompanied by criticism and punishment from his teacher. The college student, volunteering as an experimental subject, has a bright light flashed in his eyes while a tone is sounded. In both cases, particularly if the experiences are repeated, it is highly probable that behavioral changes will occur. Mathematical symbols that originally elicited no particular reaction on the part of the child, beyond, perhaps, a mild curiosity, now produce the characteristic responses of anxiety. With sufficient repetition, the sound of the tuning fork comes to elicit a pupillary contraction even though it is no longer accompanied by the flash of light. The learning process in these examples has been labeled *classical conditioning,* and the term *respondent* has been applied to the resulting behavior.

While we may say that the child has learned to fear arithmetic or that the college student has learned to respond to the tone with a pupillary contraction, notice that these responses are involuntary. They are not under the conscious control of the learner. The child can no more banish his anxiety than the college student can prevent his pupils from contracting. Parents and teachers who urge anxious children to be brave or to stop being frightened might well consider this point.

Classical conditioning has a second important characteristic. A stimulus that previously was inadequate to elicit a particular response now becomes capable of doing so. The sound of a tuning fork, though it may evoke other responses, does not ordinarily result in a pupillary contraction; nor is the sight of an arithmetic problem an unlearned stimulus for fear. However, the pairing of these inadequate stimuli with stimuli capable of giving rise to particular responses has resulted in their acquiring the capacity to evoke those responses by themselves.

In classical conditioning, whether certain stimuli occur in conjunction with one another is something over which our learners have no control. The experimenter decides whether the flash of light will be paired with the sound of the tuning fork. Whether signs of adult anger accompany arithmetic symbols is determined by the teacher, not by the child. We see the environment acting upon essentially passive subjects. Finally, these behavioral changes are not directed toward solving any particular problem, achieving any goal, or satisfying any need.

We can describe those responses that are acquired through the process of classical conditioning in terms of the following characteristics: they are involuntary; they are made in response to a previously inadequate stimulus; they result from the environment acting upon the learner; and they are not goal directed.

Psychologists, in discussing classical conditioning, speak of conditioned and unconditioned stimuli and of conditioned and unconditioned responses. Classical conditioning might be somewhat more easily understood if instead we substitute the terms *conditional* and *unconditional.*

The stimulus of a strong light directed into the eye will *unconditionally* produce the response of a pupillary contraction. The sound of a tuning fork, however, will produce a pupillary contraction only *conditionally*—that is, after it has been paired a number of times with the flash of light. We refer to the sound of the tuning fork, therefore, as a conditioned (conditional) stimulus and the response to this stimulus as a conditioned (conditional) response.

It is not safe to assume that the conditioned response is always identical to the unconditioned response. The conditioned response, while often very similar, frequently shows some variation from the unconditioned response. The sound of the tuning fork, although it elicits a pupillary contraction, will probably not produce the blinking that accompanies the flash of light. The child's emotional response to the sight of an arithmetic problem will not be exactly the same as his response to punishment or scolding by his teacher.

Some psychologists question whether any very large portion of human behavior can be explained in terms of classical conditioning. They contend that only a few very simple responses fit the characteristics of this type of learning and that most human learning possesses a set of quite different characteristics. But we may have slighted classical conditioning in considering some important aspects of human learning. Staats and Staats have demonstrated, for example, that nonsense syllables, if learned in association with words that already possess a pleasant or an unpleasant tone, acquire the emotional significance of those words.[1] Frequently we use terms such as "good" while rewarding a child and "bad" while punishing him. It is possible that by such means we are conditioning not simply responses to certain events but also the meaning of words that accompany these events. "Bad," for example, becomes capable of arousing many of the emotional responses previously aroused only by the punishment.

1. Carolyn K. Staats and Arthur W. Staats, "Meaning Established by Classical Conditioning," *Journal of Experimental Psychology* (July 1957), pp. 74–80.

INSTRUMENTAL BEHAVIOR

Learners are not always passive, and the responses they make are not always involuntary. Very often they are actively attempting to obtain some satisfaction from their environment. A hungry youngster trying to obtain a cookie and an insecure child trying to win the attention and approval of his teacher are examples of *instrumental behavior,* or, if we speak of the process, of *instrumental conditioning.* If the hungry child knows the location of the cookie jar, he may point to it and ask an adult for a cookie, he may cry, he may drag a chair into position in an effort to reach the cookies, or he may make a number of other attempts to get what he wants. Similarly, the child who craves adult approval may try to gain it in a number of ways; some may be successful, others may be ignored or lead to punishment. Those responses that result in punishment or are ignored tend to be eliminated or reduced in frequency, while successful responses are more likely to be repeated.

Classical conditioning, as we have noted, is characterized by stimulus substitution: feelings of anxiety, once aroused by punishment and the teacher's disapproval, are now aroused by the sight of an arithmetic problem; a tone now produces a pupillary contraction that was formerly made only in response to a bright light. Instrumental conditioning, on the other hand, is characterized by *response substitution:* unsuccessful responses tend to be replaced with responses that are reinforced. If the child is unsuccessful in reaching the cookies after climbing up on a chair, he will abandon this response in favor of one that produces results.

Unlike the stimuli for the pupillary contractions of the college student and the anxiety reactions of the punished child, the stimuli for these responses are not always clearly identifiable. In many cases we can only infer the nature of the stimulus from the behavior we observe. Some stimuli, such as hunger pangs, may be internal. In addition, they are not obviously applied by someone else as in the case of classical conditioning. (What, for example, is the stimulus that prompts a child to seek adult attention?) Instrumental behavior also differs from respondent behavior in that it is voluntary and goal directed—that is, it is aimed at satisfying some need or, perhaps, at avoiding some unpleasant consequence. The learner is acting upon his environment, manipulating it, or attempting to alter it, rather than simply responding to it.

In classical conditioning, the unconditioned stimulus—the flash of light, for example, or the criticism and punishment by the teacher—both elicits the response and reinforces it. In instrumental conditioning, reinforcement can occur only if the response is made independently. If we wish a child to behave politely, we can reinforce him with a smile or a pleasant comment when he demonstrates good manners, but he must first make the desired response. The smile or kind words do not elicit the polite behavior; they can only reinforce it. By manipulating reinforcements we can change and control behavior—but only if the desired behavior first occurs. In some situations, such as learning to spell a word, there are a finite number of possible responses the learner can make, and we can greatly reduce even this number by first teaching a few rules or principles. One of the more obvious techniques of teaching is to arrange conditions in such a way as to increase the probability that a correct response will be made; then that response can be reinforced. Sometimes, however, we find our attempts to change children's behavior (particularly some aspects of their social behavior) through reinforcement thwarted by the very low probability that the desired behavior will occur in the first place.

This difficulty can be partly overcome by employing the technique of *successive approximations.* This calls for reinforcing behavior that, initially, may be only a crude approximation of the desired response. By withholding reinforcement until successive responses come closer to the ideal and by reinforcing the learner at each stage, performance is gradually "shaped" in the desired direction.

We frequently employ this procedure with small children, particularly when they are learning skills. We praise the child's first clumsy efforts at drawing pictures, catching a ball, or pronouncing words. Gradually, we withhold reinforcement until his responses are more precise. This technique of successive approximations is, however, equally applicable to older learners and to such cognitive learning tasks as concept formation or problem solving.

REINFORCEMENT

Reinforcement has been mentioned several times as one of the variables affecting learning. What, exactly, do we mean by reinforcement, and what is its role in learning?

Reinforcement is usually defined as any stimulus event that increases or maintains the strength of a response. This is an operational definition of reinforcement and calls for no assumptions as to *how* reinforcement strengthens a response or what changes take place within the organism. Nor does it equate reinforcement with reward. It simply describes what reinforcement does, and many psychologists have been willing to let the matter rest there.

If we consider the behavior of a rat in a Skinner box pressing a bar to obtain food or a child trying to fit the pieces of a puzzle together, we can perhaps gain some additional knowledge of the ways in which reinforcement is related to learning. If pressing the bar produces food and if the child is able to locate and fit pieces of the puzzle together readily, both child and rat will persist in their behaviors until the food is exhausted, the puzzle completed, or both are satiated. If the rat fails to obtain food or the child, after many trials, finds no pieces that fit, each is likely to change its response. The rat may begin to investigate or gnaw at other parts of the box; the child may try sorting out pieces on the basis of shape, perhaps, rather than color, or he may abandon the puzzle entirely.

The behaviors of both rat and child suggest two functions of reinforcement: an informational function that provides feedback on successful and unsuccessful responses and a motivational function that keeps the learner at the task. When we say to a student, "That's a very good answer," we are probably increasing his general tendency to respond in class, and we are also indicating to him that this particular response is the one he should make in this particular situation.

Reinforcement need not always be pleasant or rewarding, however. Behavior can also be modified by failures or by unpleasant results. We refer to such aversive stimuli as *negative reinforcers.* But do unpleasant consequences fit our earlier definition of reinforcement? Do they, for example, increase or maintain the strength of a response? Do they motivate and provide feedback?

If a child pushes a bobby pin into an electric outlet after being warned not to do so, there will almost certainly be a change in his behavior. The consequences, if he survives them, do not strengthen the response of putting bobby pins into electric outlets. However, the weak avoidance tendencies aroused by the warning to let electric outlets alone have been greatly strengthened. His staying-away-from-electrical-outlets behavior has been strongly reinforced, and he has received some information about the inappropriateness of his original response.

Obviously, this child has learned. As a result of his experience, his behavior has changed. It is easy to conclude from such an example that learning is the *result* of reinforcement and, perhaps, to go on to the further conclusion that learning occurs *only* if the learner is reinforced. Are such conclusions warranted? Scores of experiments have demonstrated that reinforcement affects performance; but does it affect learning? Is it possible for learning to occur without reinforcement?

The designs of most of the experiments about which we read incorporate some form of reinforcement. Because of this we may be inclined to assume that reinforcement *is* necessary if learning is to occur. Most psychologists, however, argue that reinforcement affects performance directly but learning only indirectly. When a response is made, the consequences affect the learner's tendency to make that response again. Thus, reinforcement may determine what the learner does. By determining what he *does,* reinforcement may indirectly determine what he *learns.* While doing does affect learning, common sense tells us that what an individual has learned is not always reflected in what he does. There is a great deal of experimental evidence to support this belief. Furthermore, this evidence suggests that learning and performance are not affected in the same way by reinforcement.

Research has shown that learning is usually independent of the amount of reinforcement, while performance may not be.[2] If animals are minimally reinforced—if reinforcement is just sufficient to keep them responding—they ordinarily will not reach the same final level of performance as animals receiving a greater amount of reinforcement. However, there is no difference in the rates at which they learn. Furthermore, if the amount of reinforcement is increased, these minimally reinforced animals show an immediate change in their performance, indicating that learning has already occurred but is not reflected in performance until there is some reason for the animal to perform at a higher level.

---

2. B. Reynolds, "The Acquisition of a Black-White Discrimination Under Two Levels of Reinforcement," *Journal of Experimental Psychology,* Vol. XXXIX (1948), pp. 760–69; and D. Zeaman, "Response Latency as a Function of the Amount of Reinforcement," *Journal of Experimental Psychology,* Vol. XXXIX (1949), pp. 466–83.

Psychologists, attempting to test the idea that reinforcement determines performance but has little or no direct effect upon learning, have also compared learning under reinforcement with learning under no reinforcement. In one of the better-known experiments,[3] Buxton allowed rats to remain in a maze and explore it freely for several days but did not feed them in the maze. Later, they and a control group were placed directly in the goal box at the end of the maze and fed there. When placed in the start box, the rats who had previously explored the maze made significantly fewer errors in getting from the start box to the goal box, even though they had never been reinforced with food for following this particular path. What is particularly worth noting about these results is that the experimental group showed improved performance, indicating that learning had occurred *before* they were reinforced for negotiating the maze.

Human beings often exhibit similar behavior. While shopping for a pair of shoes, we may recall the location of a shoe store we passed weeks before while out for a stroll. Such unreinforced learning has been termed *latent learning,* because the learning, although it has occurred, is latent (not evident) until some incentive is introduced.

However, learning without reinforcement, although possible, is often slow and inefficient. If the learner is not reinforced frequently, particularly in the early stages of learning, he may be confused about the associations to be made. Even partial reinforcement may introduce an element of uncertainty, and, lacking the feedback provided by consistent reinforcement, he may not be able to judge and correct his responses. In simple learning tasks there may be little difference between reinforced and unreinforced learning, but in complex tasks the learner may not persist long enough or perform frequently enough without reinforcement to acquire the necessary responses. By determining what the learner does, reinforcement may indirectly determine what he learns.

But outside the laboratory we rarely have to choose between reinforcing a learner promptly for every response or not reinforcing him at all. We are more likely to be concerned with such questions as: What will happen if I reinforce this student only occasionally?

---

3. C. D. Buxton, "Latent Learning and the Goal Gradient Hypothesis," *Contributions to Psychological Theory,* Vol. II, No. 6 (1940).

Will it make any difference if I am inconsistent—if I make changes in the frequency, amount, or quality of reinforcement? What effect will it have upon learning if I delay reinforcement?

As these questions imply, there are a variety of schedules of reinforcement that we can apply. We can, for example, reinforce every response or every tenth response, or we can use almost any other ratio of responses to reinforcement. We can reinforce only those responses that occur at the end of some fixed time interval, or we can reinforce on a random basis. We can also vary the amount, intensity, or quality of the individual reinforcements.

Research on the effects of different schedules of reinforcement indicates that we can manipulate reinforcement to produce marked changes in behavior. We can produce behavior that is highly resistant to extinction or relatively easy to extinguish. Individuals reinforced on one type of schedule will show a series of peaks in their performance followed by intervals during which they make few responses. Other schedules of reinforcement result in an even, steady rate of response.

It is apparent that regulating reinforcement gives us an effective means of controlling performance. But we should not assume that by controlling performance we are directly controlling learning. What we are really controlling through reinforcement is the activity of the organism. As we have noted, activity does not inevitably lead to learning. Nor is activity essential for all types of learning. If it were, we would never learn anything from reading a book, attending a lecture, or watching a demonstration.

Delay in reinforcement, unlike changes in amount, frequency, or quality of reinforcement, does have a direct effect upon both learning and performance. A long delay between response and reinforcement acts in much the same manner as complete absence of reinforcement. A lag between a response and its consequences may deprive the learner of the feedback by which he can judge his response. And delay in reinforcing a response can affect the rate of learning by reducing the number of times the response is attempted. With laboratory animals, delaying reinforcement by even a few seconds may mean that no learning occurs. Even human subjects are badly handicapped by short delays. What is sometimes worse, if reinforcement is delayed, inappropriate responses may be learned.

Let us assume that we wish to teach a dog to sit up on command

and that we reinforce each successful effort with a bit of food. If we introduce a long delay between response and reinforcement, this interval permits the dog to make such additional responses as barking or waving his forelegs. These irrelevant acts, since they are followed by the reinforcement, may become a well-established part of the dog's total response. He sits up when we command him to do so, but he also barks and paws at the air. His performance indicates that he has made a faulty association between response and reinforcement. Skinner has termed such unnecessary responses "superstitious" behavior.[4]

Similar behavior may occur in human beings when delays in reinforcement result in uncertainty about which response is being reinforced. After taking an examination, a pupil may refuse to talk about it. Later he receives a high mark and concludes that it may have been because he didn't talk about the exam, that talking about exams may "spoil your luck."

SECONDARY REINFORCEMENT

Although delaying reinforcement for only a short time usually reduces its effectiveness, in some situations reinforcements seem to retain their efficiency even after long delays. The explanation of this puzzling state of affairs lies in another principle of learning, the principle of *secondary reinforcement.*

Some stimuli, such as food, water, or electric shock, are termed *primary reinforcers.* They appear to function as reinforcers without prior learning. Other stimuli, known as *secondary reinforcers,* acquire the capacity to reinforce behavior as a result of being associated with stimuli that already have reinforcing qualities.

If, for example, we pair punishment repeatedly with the word "nasty," we can classically condition a child so that "nasty" arouses many of the anxiety reactions previously aroused by punishment. Suppose we now pair this word with any stimuli that arouse the child's interest in sex. Eventually such stimuli as a picture of a nude figure or the words "naked" or "breast" will give rise to feelings of anxiety, even though they have never been directly associated with punishment.

---

4. B. F. Skinner, "Superstition in the Pigeon," *Journal of Experimental Psychology* (April 1948), pp. 168–72.

Secondary reinforcement applies also to instrumental conditioning. We can, for example, reinforce a dog with food while repeating "Good dog." If we continue to pair food and words, "good dog" will come to serve as a reinforcement for retrieving a ball, coming when called, or for any other instrumental response the dog is capable of making.

But how does the concept of secondary reinforcement explain the fact that delaying reinforcement does not always have an adverse effect upon learning and performance?

In some situations, even though the primary reinforcement is delayed, some form of secondary reinforcement is present. In learning a maze, rats will often continue to perform well even though they are not fed for some time after entering the goal box. Apparently, the goal box itself, having previously been associated with eating, serves as a secondary reinforcement for maze running.

Most of the stimuli that serve as secondary reinforcements for human behavior are verbal or symbolic. As we labor at some difficult or boring task, with many hours of work still ahead before we can relax or before we are "paid off," we tell ourselves, "At four o'clock I'll *rest*." Or we think, "If I can learn this, I'll get *a good grade*." Because of previous associations the word "rest" and the symbol of a grade have acquired the capacity to reinforce our behavior and to bridge the gap between present activities and some long-delayed reinforcement, such as actual rest or parental rewards for academic achievement.

Secondary reinforcement is important in explaining a major portion of human behavior, because so few of our responses are directly reinforced with food, water, or other primary reinforcers. To reinforce human behavior we rely heavily upon knowledge of results, social status, money, and a variety of symbolic rewards and punishments.

EXTINCTION AND SPONTANEOUS RECOVERY

It is apparent that it is not necessary to reinforce every response in order to keep an organism responding. Hunters come home empty handed after hours in icy duck blinds, only to return again and again. Parents complain of the lasting effects on their children's behavior of an occasional weekend with indulgent grandparents. And psychologists can offer evidence from research with both animal and human subjects that partial or intermittent reinforcement produces more persistent behavior than does reinforcing every response.

Nevertheless, if reinforcement is withheld long enough, the duck hunter, the child, or the laboratory animal will finally cease to respond. We refer to this disappearance of the response as *extinction.* Superficially, extinction appears to be a rather simple state of affairs, and we may be inclined to dismiss it by assuming that organisms stop responding because they aren't "getting anything out of it." This explanation, however, leaves many questions unanswered.

One gets very little out of conditioned pupillary contraction, and the child who fears arithmetic derives little pleasure from his anxieties. Why do these responses not disappear immediately once reinforcement is withdrawn? Why does partial reinforcement result in behavior that is resistant to extinction? How can we explain the apparently spontaneous reappearance of responses that seemed to have been thoroughly eliminated? Since a considerable share of our educational efforts are aimed at eliminating undesirable behavior and at teaching children *not* to respond under many circumstances, these questions about extinction are worth our attention.

What does happen when reinforcement is withdrawn and a particular behavior is extinguished? Does a process of "unlearning" take place? Or is the old response displaced by some competing response?

There are several possible explanations of what happens when reinforcement is withdrawn. One, already mentioned, is that the organism simply refuses to respond unless reinforced. This does not provide a very satisfactory explanation for the extinction of responses previously established through classical conditioning, since such responses are not under voluntary control. Nor is it a completely satisfactory explanation for the extinction of instrumental behavior. Reinforcement of the instrumental responses of human beings is rarely as mechanical and obvious as the reinforcement of a rat in a Skinner box. Few of us go skiing or avoid talking to strangers because we are aware that these behaviors are being reinforced. We usually have vague feelings of pleasure, satisfaction, or absence of tension, which we may not connect directly with the response. Our reasons for ceasing to make a particular response are often equally vague.

Another possible explanation of extinction is that a process of "unlearning" takes place when we withdraw reinforcement. Unfortunately for this explanation, if we allow a period of time to pass during which we make no attempt to evoke the extinguished behavior and then once again present the stimulus, we may see the response reappear. This phenomenon, known as *spontaneous recovery,* demonstrates that, while the response disappeared during extinction, it was not entirely eliminated or "unlearned."

Extinction has also been explained as a matter of learning a competing response—that is, when reinforcement is withdrawn, the learner acquires a response of withholding or of "not doing so." He becomes conditioned to inhibit his previous response. This *conditioned-inhibition theory* is simple and economical. It introduces no new processes and explains extinction as the result of learning a new response that competes successfully with the old response. However, if learning and extinction are the same process, they should be affected similarly by the same variables. They are not. Massing practice trials, for example, retards learning, but massing unreinforced trials accelerates extinction. The phenomenon of spontaneous recovery also gives rise to another objection to the conditioned-inhibition theory. It leaves us with the question of what happens to this competing response when spontaneous recovery of the original response occurs. Why should a period of nonstimulation result in the disappearance of the competing response?

Clark Hull offered an explanation of extinction that combined the concept of conditioned inhibition with another form of inhibition, which he referred to as *reactive inhibition.*[5] Hull believed that each response increases the tendency not to make the same response in the immediate future. Each of us has experienced the apparent fatigue that results from doing the same thing over and over. After a time we begin to develop a strong desire to do something else, and our performance frequently begins to decline. According to Hull, this "fatigue" is the result of reactive inhibition, and extinction occurs when there is no reinforcement to offset this effect.

It can be shown, however, that rest following extinction does not bring a response back in its original strength. If extinction were

5. C. L. Hull, *The Principles of Learning* (New York: Appleton-Century-Crofts, 1943), pp. 269–72.

due to the fatiguing effects of responding without reinforcement, the extinguished response should recover its original strength after a rest period of sufficient length. It does not do so. Spontaneous recovery following extinction almost always results in a response with less than 50 percent of its original strength. Hull explained this lack of complete recovery as the result of the additional factor of conditioned inhibition. Reactive inhibition, according to Hull, disappears with rest, but conditioned inhibition does not, resulting in a less than complete recovery of response strength.

Both the conditioned-inhibition theory of extinction and Hull's two-factor theory are based upon the assumption that extinction is response induced. This should mean that, if we can arrange conditions so that an organism is stimulated to make a response but the response does not actually occur, that particular response should not be extinguished no matter how many times the stimulus is presented. Yet extinction can occur under just such circumstances. In the case of a child who fears the dark, for example, we can resort to subliminal stimulation, to stimulation of such low intensity that it does not quite evoke a response. We can dim the light in his bedroom by imperceptible degrees over an extended period of time until, eventually, complete darkness no longer evokes fear. Horse trainers sometimes employ a similar technique by putting increasingly heavy weights upon the back of a horse, being careful that each increase is not sufficient to trigger a bucking response.

Parents who permit the baby to "cry it out" are employing a second type of stimulation-without-response. They are allowing stimulation to continue beyond the point where any further response is possible. The baby eventually becomes so fatigued that, although the stimuli for crying are still present, he can no longer respond to them.

We can also stimulate the individual under conditions that do not permit him to respond. Teachers and mothers with marked fears of snakes or mice sometimes find themselves in situations where they must appear poised and calm under the scrutiny of their children. They cannot respond typically, and if this situation is repeated a number of times mice and snakes may lose their capacity for evoking the responses of fear and flight.

Such examples suggest the possibility that extinction may be stimulus induced rather than response induced. It may be that we do not so much tire of responding as we tire of the same old stimulus. Support for this *stimulus-satiation* explanation of extinction can be found in the classroom as well as in the laboratory. Quite frequently, by changing the stimulus slightly we can bring about the reappearance of extinguished behavior. A new textbook, for instance, even though it contains much the same material as the old one, may revive student interest and effort. And a teacher is sometimes chagrined to find that a visitor to his class, even though he may discuss the same topics the teacher has been discussing and perhaps discuss them less skillfully, is accorded rapt attention and is freely quoted for days afterward.

The relationship of stimulation to extinction is apparent in other ways. Responses that are learned under distracting conditions tend to show a decreased resistance to extinction. While human beings do possess a remarkable capacity to ignore stimulation that is not damaging or painful, this particular effect of distracting stimuli on learning is something to be borne in mind by those who study with a radio playing and by teachers who permit excessive noise and confusion in their classrooms. The occurrence of extraneous, distracting stimuli during extinction trials seems to increase resistance to extinction. This effect, known as *disinhibition,* may be due to the subject giving only partial attention to the critical stimulus. Consequently, stimulus satiation may develop less rapidly. Whether we are interested in the acquisition of a response or in extinguishing some unwanted behavior, a nondistracting environment seems desirable.

Although our understanding of extinction is incomplete, it seems probable that extinction is not the result of a single process. Both repeated stimulation and repeated responding seem to produce an inhibitory effect, which results in extinction unless offset by reinforcement, rest, or changes in stimulation. In other cases it seems clear that a response has been extinguished as the result of having learned a new, competing response or of having learned to do nothing. In the case of the teacher who must handle snakes or mice in front of students, extinction may be the result of a combination of stimulus satiation and learning the competing response of handling these animals.

Attempts to explain extinction are complicated by another factor: withdrawal of reinforcement sometimes results in emotional reactions that indirectly affect performance. Human beings, as we all know, frequently show signs of frustration when their expectations are violated. It is always risky to attribute to other organisms the perceptions and reactions of human beings, but many experimenters have noted that animals do show signs of excitement when reinforcement is withdrawn. This excitation may offset the effects of withdrawing reinforcement and result, temporarily, in increased performance. Moreover, the closer the animal is allowed to get to an anticipated reinforcement before that reinforcement is withdrawn, the more difficult it becomes to extinguish the behavior.

Expectation of reinforcement has also been used as a basis for explaining why partial reinforcement results in persistent behavior. The organism's expectations, it is contended, are not violated when no reinforcement occurs, because not every response was reinforced during learning. Another related explanation makes use of the concept of *response units.* According to this explanation, if we reinforce a subject each time he responds, one reinforcement per response will be the response unit. If, however, we reinforce him at the rate of ten responses per reinforcement, the response unit will be one reinforcement per ten responses. In other words, it is assumed that he reacts as though each of these ten separate responses were really a part of a total response that results in reinforcement. Extinction following partial reinforcement might require more unreinforced individual responses than extinction following 100 percent reinforcement but approximately the same number of unreinforced response units.

In addition to their implications for modifying behavior, studies of extinction and spontaneous recovery suggest that learning is relatively stable and enduring, whereas performance is affected by such transitory factors as the presence of appropriate stimulation, fatigue, motivation, and reinforcement. By withholding reinforcement, for example, we may extinguish performance, but we do not extinguish learning. Learning that seems to have been eliminated may reappear with a change in stimulation or in reinforcement. Our previous definition of learning, therefore, is in need of modification: learning is not simply a change in behavior but a relatively permanent change in ability to perform or in behavior potential that may be manifested only in some long-delayed change in behavior.

LEARNING CHARACTERISTICS AND TEACHING

The preceding discussion is not intended to provide an exhaustive description of the characteristics of learned behavior. Such a description is beyond the scope of this book. Nor is it an attempt to distill a large and complex body of knowledge into a series of prescriptions for teaching. Some general implications for teaching are, of course, fairly apparent: the importance of providing for prompt reinforcement and the possibility of controlling behavior through reinforcement; the usefulness of the technique of successive approximations in shaping performance; the futility of expecting students to exert voluntary control over responses established through classical conditioning; the importance of secondary reinforcement as an explanation for much otherwise-puzzling behavior.

However, the major purpose of discussing the characteristics of learning has been to provide a point of view, a theoretical framework, and a set of principles that will be helpful in thinking about other aspects of learning: about motivation, retention, or transfer; about such questions as the manner in which verbal behavior develops, how human beings acquire concepts, develop skills, or learn to solve problems.

Every teacher is faced each day with the necessity of making a great many decisions. Teaching might very well be described as a process of making decisions about human behavior: Should this particular child be called upon? Is that response acceptable? Should I remain silent or offer an explanation? How can this topic best be introduced? Each of these questions calls for a decision, and each decision is, in effect, an hypothesis about human behavior. It is a prediction—sometimes a guess—that if certain things are done certain consequences will follow.

Often our decisions turn out well. A lagging discussion becomes more lively, a student seems to grasp an explanation that had eluded him, or an underachiever begins to work up to his capacity. Teachers, too, respond to reinforcement. If our decisions lead to the desired results we usually repeat them when similar circumstances arise; but, unless we have some systematic way of viewing human behavior, relying solely on past experience as a guide has certain shortcomings.

Two situations are rarely identical in all respects, and we may overlook subtle but critical differences, with the result that the same teacher behaviors may not result in the same student responses. Moreover, if we rely on the trial and error of experience, we may be successful without really understanding why. It is helpful to have a repertoire of effective teaching techniques, but even experienced teachers are constantly encountering new problems. A theoretical model of learning may help us organize our perceptions and focus our attention on the important variables in any learning situation. It may also help us understand why a particular procedure has been effective and thus enable us to decide whether it will be equally effective in some new situation.

A theoretical explanation of learning can also be useful in helping us go beyond our own experiences to develop reasonable hypotheses rather than mere guesses. For example, many adults, although they often engage in similar behavior themselves, are baffled and annoyed when students spend a great deal of time sharpening pencils, organizing their notebooks, and clearing off their desks instead of studying for a test. Why do so many students waste badly needed study time in this way?

We can advance a number of explanations for this behavior: the students don't really care about their performance on the test; the importance of tests has not been sufficiently emphasized by the teacher; they do not know how to organize their time. Each of these explanations suggests steps we might take that would change this behavior. We could lecture them on the importance of good grades, give tests more frequently, and emphasize test results in determining grades. Or we might organize a course in study skills.

However, in talking with students, we usually discover that the majority of them are concerned about tests; they are, in fact, often extremely anxious about their performance. Frequently, their anxiety seems to stem from an existing emphasis on tests. We may also find that, while their study habits are not very good, they seem to know how they should study. Our first hypotheses about this behavior are apparently not supported by our data. Consequently, there is good reason to question whether remedial procedures based on these hypotheses will really be effective. Is there some other reasonable explanation for this behavior, some explanation that might suggest some effective decisions we might make?

We might first assume that the simplest explanation may be the correct one: these students are telling the truth—they do know how to study, the results of the examination are important to them, and their basic problem is anxiety. But, if they really are concerned about their grades and if they know how to study, why do they not settle down to studying? Why do they continue to waste time on these nonessential tasks?

Anxiety reactions can be disorganizing, and we know that these reactions, like other emotional responses, are examples of respondent behavior. They are not under the individual's voluntary control. Therefore, lecturing and criticizing or further instruction in study techniques will not be effective in changing this response. But, although these students are anxious and cannot simply decide not to be anxious, they could engage in instrumental behavior aimed at reducing anxiety. They could study; why don't they?

Studying probably would result in increased confidence and decreased anxiety about the examination. But even thinking about studying raises the anxiety-provoking specter of the examination. Sharpening pencils, on the other hand, results in at least mild feelings of accomplishment. Tidying desks and organizing notebooks has been praised in the past and also has some secondary reinforcing power. More significantly, these activities serve to distract them from the threat of the examination, and anxiety reduction is a potent reinforcer. Since they are being reinforced, these activities are likely to persist unless the threat of the examination becomes so overwhelming that the resulting anxiety cannot be reduced sufficiently in this way. In the meantime, of course, valuable time has been lost, and anxiety levels may have reached the point where they seriously interfere with learning.

This explanation has certain advantages over our previous explanations. First, and most important, it fits the data. It also suggests some ways in which we might deal with the behavior. We might, for example, attempt to extinguish anxiety or reduce it to manageable levels by giving tests more frequently, while placing less emphasis upon the results. Or we might examine our tests or our instructional procedures. Students may be anxious because they have really learned very little and feel unprepared or because our tests may be too difficult, poorly constructed, or perhaps not closely related to the content of our course.

This explanation of a phase of student behavior has the additional value of being based on an approach that is applicable to other situations in which human behavior may appear, at least on the surface, to be quite irrational. When we encounter such problems we should seek an explanation, as we have in this case, based on an understanding of the nature of the responses being made and a consideration of the conditions that probably arouse and maintain these responses.

As this discussion of one particular pattern of student behavior illustrates, a knowledge of the characteristics of learning does not give us direct, simple answers to the problem of understanding human behavior. It does, however, provide us with tools for evaluating our experiences critically.

But tools are not enough; nor is it enough to be able to distinguish between respondent and instrumental behavior or to grasp the concept of reinforcement. We must be able to apply our knowledge imaginatively if we are to think intelligently and productively about human learning. Our task, however, is not one of application in the obvious sense of the word. Some psychological concepts, as we have seen, are useful to the teacher, and the results of psychological experiments, even with animals, are often sources of important hypotheses about human learning. But it is more important that we derive from psychology a sensitivity to the world of behavioral events, a habit of thought that causes us to observe carefully, to raise questions about behavior, and to attempt to answer these questions in a systematic manner. Conceiving teaching in this way can make it a creative and intellectually challenging activity, raising it above the level of a craft and raising teachers above the level of classroom technicians.

Suggestions for Class Discussion and Further Investigation

1. How would you reply to the statement "It may be a good theory of learning, but it can't be applied to teaching"?
2. Evaluate the statement "Teaching is an art; therefore, we can never have a science of education."
3. Programed materials have not been notably effective in teaching people to be original or creative. Is this simply a technical limitation on programed instruction, or are creativity and originality not learned in the same way other responses are learned?
4. Evaluate the following statements about learning:

(*a*) Learning depends on reward and punishment.
(*b*) Learning should be fun.
(*c*) Learning is "being told."
(*d*) Pavlov's dog learned to salivate.

5. Consider one of your own habits or responses. To what are you responding? Can you describe the process by which you acquired this response? How would you go about extinguishing this behavior?
6. Ask two classmates or friends to serve as subjects for the following experiment:
   (*a*) Blindfold your first subject, and then tell him that you are going to draw a line between three and six inches long on a piece of paper and that he is to draw a line of the same length. Draw your line several inches long and then have him try to produce a line of equal length. After each trial say only "yes" if his line is within one-fourth inch of yours or "no" if his line is not of the required length. Count the number of trials required to produce two lines of correct length.
   (*b*) Use the same procedure with the second subject, but this time after each unsuccessful trial say, "No, a little longer (or shorter)."
   Compare the performance of the two subjects. What are the shortcomings of this experiment?
7. Would you agree with the statement that good teaching is primarily a matter of arranging conditions so as to elicit the desired response?

Suggestions for Further Reading

Sarnoff A. Mednick's short (118-page) paperback, *Learning* (Englewood Cliffs, N.J.: Prentice-Hall, Foundations of Modern Psychology Series, 1964), while drawing largely on research with animals, offers a highly readable discussion of the basic principles of learning.

Teaching machines and programed materials represent the most direct application of instrumental conditioning principles to learning. For two contrasting views of how these principles should be applied to the actual construction of programs, see B. F. Skinner, "Teaching Machines," and Norman A. Crowder,

"The Rationale of Intrinsic Programming." Both appear in John P. DeCecco, ed., *Human Learning in the School* (New York: Holt, Rinehart and Winston, 1963).

Although they take different approaches, both Robert M. Gagné in his *The Conditions of Learning* (New York: Holt, Rinehart and Winston, 1965), and B. R. Bugelski in his *The Psychology of Learning Applied to Teaching* (Indianapolis, Ind.: Bobbs-Merrill, 1964), skillfully translate psychological principles into educational practices. Gagné attempts to identify what he regards as different types of learning and then to describe the conditions under which each type occurs. Bugelski traces the influences and applications of three traditions: the Thorndike tradition with the representative theories of Hull and Skinner; the Pavlovian tradition as exemplified in the theories of Watson, Guthrie, and Tolman; and O. A. Mowrer's integration of these two traditions. This is an interesting and useful book both for the student who wishes a comparison of the major theories of learning and for the teacher who wonders if there is any application of learning theory to teaching.

Although Vincent Dethier is a physiologist with primary interest in animal behavior rather than a psychologist or an educator, his book, *To Know a Fly* (San Francisco: Holden-Day, 1962), should impress any reader with the fact that it is possible to carry on scientific inquiry with little or no equipment, provided one uses intelligence and imagination. It may surprise many readers to find that it is possible to write amusingly and entertainingly about research.

Chapter Three

Motivation: Basic Concepts

Teachers and parents talk a great deal about motivation, and they use the term in a bewildering variety of ways. Parents complain that teachers fail to motivate their children, implying that motivating is something that one person does to another. Teachers remark that children are lacking in motivation, suggesting that motivation is some characteristic or condition of the learner. And both parents and teachers agree that many children aren't strongly motivated in science or mathematics, suggesting that motivation may be a function of a particular situation.

When a term can be used in so many different ways, we wonder whether it helps or hinders our thinking. There is a very real danger that when we employ a hazy redefinition of some aspect of behavior we are left with a spurious sense of having explained it when we have simply relabeled it. A guidance counselor who describes a student's problem as "a lack of motivation for college work" is really not telling us much more than the teacher who says the student is failing because he will not work. One psychologist, George Kelly, believes we could get along very well without the concept of motivation,[1] and Skinner has suggested that we may have created a "linguistic fiction." [2] Bugelski has observed that so-called definitions of motivation are not really definitions but statements about a particular area of discourse and that " 'motivation' is not an entity or a 'force' but an expression referring to a wide variety of conditions which alter stimulus-response relationships." [3]

1. George A. Kelly, "Man's Construction of His Alternatives," in Gardner Lindzey, ed., *The Assessment of Human Motives* (New York: Holt, Rinehart and Winston, 1958), pp. 33–64.
2. Quoted in B. R. Bugelski, *The Psychology of Learning* (New York: Holt, Rinehart and Winston, 1956), p. 241.
3. *Ibid.*

Since motivation has been defined so imprecisely, it is not surprising to find much disagreement among psychologists about motivation or to find that they have taken different approaches in studying it. Several general views of motivation do emerge, however. Some psychologists prefer to view motivation as arising from an internal imbalance of the organism. For them, motivation can be explained on the basis of unlearned physiological needs. Presumably, when these needs are unsatisfied, the resulting physiological imbalances lead to excitation of the central nervous system. This central-neural excitation that the organism experiences is referred to as a *drive*. Drive states result in general activity, which eventually leads to drive reduction and learning. The concept of drive reduction has been for many years the basis of dominant theory of motivation.

Other psychologists have preferred to explain motivation as a matter of external stimulation arousing behavior. From this viewpoint, we can motivate organisms by manipulating incentives—by increasing the amount or quality of a reward or varying the schedule of "payoffs" for performance. Most psychologists who take this view of motivation acknowledge that receptivity to a given incentive depends upon an organism's internal state. Food obviously is a more effective incentive for a hungry animal than for one that is satiated. But, they argue, while we can deprive animals of food, we cannot really know what occurs within the animal as a result of this deprivation. Consequently, they believe we should attempt to explain motivation in terms of observable external events and not resort to hypothetical constructs, such as needs and drives.

A more extreme position has been taken by other psychologists who contend that drive reduction simply does not offer an adequate explanation of motivation. Some stimuli, they argue, are motivating, not because they are associated with the reduction of some drive, but because they have satisfying psychological consequences —it "feels good" when certain responses are made, even though no physiological need is being satisfied. They point out that rats with an electrode implanted in a specific portion of the brain will work energetically at pressing a bar in order to receive a mild electrical stimulation of this "pleasure center." Harry Harlow, who has objected to a drive-reduction theory of motivation, reports that infant monkeys, although fed on a surrogate mother made of wire mesh, preferred to spend their time clasping a nonfeeding, terrycloth-covered mother figure.[4]

Although it is difficult to see in what manner the bar pressing of the rats serves to reduce any drive, the cuddling behavior of Harlow's infant monkeys can be explained in drive-reduction terms. Warm-blooded animals have a need to maintain body temperature within narrow limits if they are to survive, and this capacity for temperature regulation develops rather slowly in most young mammals, infant monkeys included. The terrycloth-covered figure may indeed "feel good" to the baby monkey, but it also has a much greater capacity than the wire-mesh figure to prevent excessive loss of body heat. Harlow's observations are not, therefore, necessarily in conflict with a drive-reduction theory of motivation.

Unfortunately, neither drive-reduction incentive explanations nor strictly hedonistic views of motivation have yielded much in the way of principles or information immediately useful to teachers, parents, or others interested in human motivation. Much of the research on motivation has utilized animals as subjects, and it is usually only under exceptional circumstances that we are able to subject human beings to food, water, or sexual deprivation experimentally—and then usually only adult subjects. Even if such experiments could be performed more readily, it seems unlikely that the results would be very useful to teachers or parents, since they are scarcely in a position to employ such deprivations as motivational techniques. In any case, it seems doubtful that any major part of human behavior can be explained solely in terms of the reduction of physiological drives. In many human societies, including our own, even eating cannot be explained entirely on the basis of the reduction of hunger. We eat because we are hungry; but we also eat sometimes because we wish to be polite, because we are upset, or because we have become accustomed to eating at a particular time of day.

Research on human drive reduction has encountered serious difficulties because of this ability of human beings to acquire additional needs through learning. Many human "needs" are clearly the result of learning. No one needs a new car, power over other

---

4. H. F. Harlow, "The Nature of Love," *American Psychologist* (December 1958), pp. 673–85.

human beings, or the respect of his friends in the same sense that he needs food, water, or protection from temperature fluctuations. Such "needs" are learned; but we sometimes work even harder to satisfy them than to satisfy our physiological needs. Which means, of course, that a comprehensive explanation of the behavior of any human being in terms of drive reduction would require a far more detailed knowledge of his learning history than we are likely to be able to obtain.

Similar problems arise in motivation research based on an external-stimulus approach, once again because of the capacity of human subjects to respond to a wide range of symbols that, through secondary reinforcement, have acquired the capacity to reinforce behavior. Animals, as we have noted, do respond to secondary reinforcers; but the behavior of animals is not an ideal basis from which to generalize to human motivation, since animals respond to a much more limited range of reinforcing stimuli.

Choosing between drive reduction or external stimulation as the basis for explaining motivation is not a matter of choosing between opposing theories. It is a question of whether we wish to stress external, observable events or internal, hypothetical states. Some behaviors do not occur unless the appropriate external stimulus is present. For example, animals do not ordinarily engage in actual eating, drinking, or sexual behavior unless food, liquid, or some sexual object is present. On the other hand, some external stimuli will evoke a response only if a particular drive state exists. We can manipulate the behavior of a hungry subject by changing the amounts or the schedule we use in reinforcing him with food. But the fact remains that if he is satiated he is not much inclined to engage in behavior that serves no other purpose than the obtaining of food, regardless of how we arrange or manage this incentive. Some psychologists have preferred to stress reinforcement variables; others have chosen to consider the question of why the organism responds to the reinforcement.

DRIVE APPROACHES

The basis for a drive-reduction theory of motivation is the concept of *homeostasis,* the idea that organisms seek to maintain some optimal physiological state. When some imbalance develops—a change in blood chemistry, dehydration, a drop in body temperature—the organism is aroused to activity. This *drive state* is maintained until the particular need is reduced through restoration of physiological balance. Drive reduction serves to reinforce those behaviors that precede it, and we may say that the organism has *learned* to find food or water or to seek shelter from the cold.

Using the concept of secondary reinforcement, we can build an explanation of the acquisition of many other needs. The restless, fretful behavior of the hungry infant, for example, is noted by his mother, who feeds him. She also holds him and talks to him. This stimulation, being associated with food (which is itself an unlearned reinforcement), comes to have reinforcing properties, and the child eventually engages in behavior aimed at getting his mother to talk to him and hold him even when he is not hungry. Thus, we can explain certain behaviors of the child as being motivated by an acquired need for attention or affection. Similarly, we can explain the development of needs for achievement, self-esteem, and other learned needs. The combination of drive reduction and secondary reinforcement offers a variety of possibilities for the manipulation and control of behavior, since additional needs and the drives arising from them should result in new or additional behavior aimed at reduction of these acquired drives.

Unfortunately, when we attempt to explain a particular behavior in terms of drive reduction and secondary reinforcement, we sometimes find ourselves confronted with a number of conflicting explanations. What motivates a man to buy health insurance? Does his action derive from a need to avoid pain, danger, and threats to his well-being by assuring himself of good medical care if he should need it? Perhaps. But we might also conjecture that his behavior is related to a need for self-esteem and that buying health insurance enables him to see himself as prudent, responsible, and foresighted. Another major difficulty here lies in the fact that these hypotheses not only conflict but are equally untestable.

Another serious difficulty with drive reduction as an explanation of motivation is that there is not complete agreement on the number of drives or even on which drives are unlearned. Drives with a physiological basis, such as hunger, thirst, and sex, presumably are unlearned. Is the drive to avoid painful stimuli also innate? It may appear reasonable to assume so. But when Melzak and Scott raised puppies in a "super-safe" environment designed to prevent them from experiencing any painful stimulation, they showed little inclination to avoid objects that hurt them when they were placed in a normal environment and, in fact, came into contact with such objects again and again.[5]

Data from other research, however, have been interpreted so as to add to the list of presumed innate drives. It has been found, for example, that simply being permitted to manipulate the parts of a puzzle was sufficiently reinforcing to keep monkeys at the task.[6] Others would work at discrimination tasks if reinforced by being permitted to look out a window in their box for thirty seconds after successfully completing a task.[7] On the basis of such research and data from latent learning experiments, some psychologists have postulated innate curiosity and manipulative and exploratory drives. Research on the effects of sensory deprivation on human subjects through the use of blindfolds, soundproof rooms, and the elimination, so far as possible, of tactile sensations has led other psychologists to refer to a need for stimulation or, perhaps more accurately, to a need for change in stimulation.

Of course, needs or drives, like learning and intelligence, are hypothetical constructs. They are useful in explaining certain aspects of behavior, but the psychologist studying motivation is not engaged in a search for drives in the manner of a miner searching through gravel for gold nuggets. We really explain nothing by naming new drives to account for behavior that we cannot attribute to any of the needs on existing lists. To explain that a child is motivated to do something because he has a need to do so redefines the behavior but adds little or nothing to our understanding of it.

Some of the inadequacies of a drive-reduction explanation of motivation are theoretical—that is, some motivational phenomena do not fit such a model of human motivation, or, if they are explained in drive-reduction terms, the explanation conflicts with existing principles of learning. These shortcomings of drive-reduc-

---

5. R. Melzak and T. H. Scott, "The Effects of Early Experience on the Response to Pain," *Journal of Comparative and Physiological Psychology* (April 1957), pp. 155–61.
6. H. F. Harlow, "Learning and Satiation of Response in Intrinsically Motivated Complex Puzzle Performance by Monkeys," *ibid.* (August 1950), 289–94.
7. R. A. Butler, "Discrimination Learning by Rhesus Monkeys to Visual-Exploration Motivation," *ibid.* (April 1953), pp. 95–98.

tion theory become particularly apparent when we try to explain the acquisition of needs through secondary reinforcement.

We have considered the possibility that an infant may acquire a need for affection as a result of the stimulus of an adult presence being associated with feeding and the reduction of his hunger drive. The fact of the matter is that the delay between the act of eating and any change in the physiological basis for hunger is so great that, theoretically, drive reduction probably should not serve to reinforce eating behavior. Consequently, stimuli associated with eating should not be expected to acquire any secondary reinforcing power. However, we know that human beings do acquire many needs and that a stimulus paired with eating very frequently acquires some of the satisfying properties associated with eating for human subjects. This occurs in spite of this theoretical objection.

The data obviously contradict the theory, so we must look for another explanation. Since conditioning *does* take place and these stimuli associated with eating do acquire secondary reinforcing power, it has been argued that the act of eating, itself, produces a pleasant type of stimulation and that the reinforcing effect is not due to reduction of the hunger drive but to the positive stimulus value of eating. Note that this explanation emphasizes the possibility that some stimuli—those associated with the activity of eating, for example—may be motivating because they have pleasurable consequences and not because they are immediately related to the reduction of a drive. A moderately hungry infant, for instance, may suck happily on his thumb or on a rubber pacifier.

Perhaps of more importance to our understanding of motivation than these questions of which needs are innate and which are acquired or what the total number of human needs may be is the question of whether needs serve simply as *energizers* or whether they have a *directive* function. Do they simply arouse the individual to general activity or do they also provide cues to appropriate drive-reducing behavior? Do we merely need to learn the means of attaining certain goals, or do we also need to learn that specific goal objects or events will satisfy certain needs? Experimental evidence suggests that drive conditions may function to lower thresholds for some types of stimulation, resulting in a tendency to attend to certain stimuli more than to others. When we are hungry, for example, we may show a heightened awareness of food odors or be more likely to note items of food than if we are satiated.

Hunger and other drives do make us more active. In a sense, they may also serve a directive function if they increase the probability that we will respond to stimuli capable of reducing our drive.

A less obvious, but basic, difficulty with a drive-reduction theory of motivation is that it attempts to answer the question "Why?" Why does an individual become active? Why does a student spend his time annoying his classmates? Questions of this "why" type inevitably lead us into explanations based on hypothetical constructs and untestable assumptions about presumed inner states, about needs, drives, and tensions. Cause-and-effect relationships are exceedingly difficult to establish under the best of circumstances, and most other fields of scientific inquiry have abandoned questions of "why" for questions of "what" and "when." Psychologists who are concerned about the shortcomings of drive-reduction theory contend that our time would be more profitably spent in seeking answers to questions of this latter type: When does this particular behavior occur? What are the conditions that precede and accompany this behavior?

STIMULUS APPROACHES

The complex nature of human needs and our inability to study them directly has led some psychologists to emphasize the role of external stimulation in motivation. They point out that even homeostatic imbalance can be said to have an external origin, since the deprivations producing hunger, thirst, or sexual tensions arise in the environment. Moreover, acquired needs, such as the child's need for affection and attention, develop, at least partially, through his experiences with his environment, particularly his experiences with his parents. Their principal argument, however, is that, since we can never actually see or study needs directly, we might better confine our attention to what can be investigated with reasonable directness: external stimulation and the role of reinforcement in motivation.

This approach is in a sense atheoretical; it does not necessitate any particular assumptions about underlying needs or drives, and it seeks to answer the question "What happens to behavior when we manipulate reinforcements?" Previously, we considered the effects of reinforcement upon learning. We now turn our attention to the effects of variations in reinforcement upon responses that have already been learned.

Variations in reinforcement can take a variety of forms: changes in schedules of reinforcement, differences in the amount of reinforcement, and shifts in the quality or type of reinforcement. Research has demonstrated that the schedule of reinforcement is a very important variable in controlling behavior. Teachers, therefore, should be familiar with the effects of different types of reinforcement schedules.

There are several ways in which we can manipulate schedules of reinforcement. We can regulate the *interval of time* between reinforcements and the *ratio* of responses to reinforcements. We can also decide whether reinforcements will occur on a *variable,* or random, basis or whether they will be applied on some *fixed,* or systematic, basis. These options give us the following four basic schedules of reinforcement, each of which tends to result in a characteristic pattern of performance:

1. *Variable-ratio reinforcement.* Reinforcement occurs after varying numbers of responses have been made. It is not possible for the organism to predict exactly how many responses are necessary for reinforcement, and this puts a premium upon a high, steady rate of response. Variable reinforcement is probably most similar to the conditions under which reinforcement occurs in the majority of nonexperimental situations.

2. *Fixed-ratio reinforcement.* Reinforcement occurs after a specific number of responses have been made. Since reinforcement depends upon the number of responses made, fixed-ratio schedules result in a high, but variable, rate of response. The organism reinforced on a fixed-ratio schedule typically responds rapidly until reinforced; following reinforcement the rate of response tends to decline.

3. *Variable-interval reinforcement.* Reinforcement is administered at random times. As in the case of variable-ratio reinforcement, the organism cannot be sure which response will be reinforced, so he must keep responding in order to receive a reinforcement. However, obtaining a reinforcement does not depend upon the number of responses made. As a result, under a variable-interval schedule of reinforcement, organisms tend to respond at a uniform, but moderate, rate.

4. *Fixed-interval reinforcement.* Reinforcement that is deliv-

ered on a fixed time schedule has an interesting effect upon learned behavior: organisms reinforced on such a schedule tend to make the same number of responses per reinforcement, regardless of the length of the interval between reinforcements. If, for example, an animal has been responding ten times during each five-minute interval and we double the length of the interval to ten minutes, the animal's rate of response will shift from the previous rate of two responses per minute to approximately one response per minute. The animal gives the appearance of having made a decision as to how many responses this particular reinforcement is worth. Changing the interval between reinforcements does not change the amount of effort he will expend.

In considering the effects of these schedules of reinforcement upon behavior it is important to note that they are schedules of *partial reinforcement* and that the behavior is presumably already well learned.

Partial reinforcement offers a number of advantages over reinforcing every occurrence of a response. We have noted that partial reinforcement tends to produce behavior more resistant to extinction and that considerable control can be exerted over performance by selecting schedules of reinforcement. However, we have also observed that partial reinforcement during acquisition results in a slower rate of learning. Ideally, then, we should shift the learner from a schedule of 100 percent reinforcement to some type of partial reinforcement once he has acquired the desired response. How do we shift from one schedule of reinforcement to another? More to the point, what happens when we make such a shift, and how do the effects of a change in the frequency of reinforcement compare with the effects of a change in the amount or quality of reinforcement?

Research to date can only suggest some possibilities. Based on limited evidence drawn primarily from research with animals, it would seem that a change in frequency of reinforcement has less effect than a change in the quantity or quality of reinforcement. Amsel and Roussel reported a decline in the performance of animals when the quantity of reinforcement was reduced,[8] and Young and Shuford reported similar results when the quality of the

8. A. Amsel and J. Roussel, "Motivational Properties of Frustration: I, Effect on a Running Response of the Addition of Frustration to the Motivational Complex," *Journal of Experimental Psychology* (May 1952), pp. 363–68.

incentive drink was reduced by lowering the concentration of sucrose it contained.[9] On the other hand, omitting reinforcement entirely, according to Amsel and Roussel, produced only a temporary decline or no decline at all and sometimes resulted in increased performance. They attributed this last effect to a violation of the subject's expectations, resulting in frustration and an increase in performance due to the energizing effect of this frustration.

Frustration may energize the behavior of rats and perhaps the behavior of human beings, but the danger of generalizing from animal research to the much more complex behavior of human beings is illustrated by an experiment by Waterhouse and Child.[10] They studied the effects of frustration on the performance of human subjects and concluded that the specific effects of frustration were related to personality variables. Individuals with certain traits showed a decline in performance under frustrating conditions, while the performance of others improved. Moreover, the relative efficiency of the two groups was reversed under nonfrustrating conditions.

What are the effects on performance of different kinds of reinforcement? As we noted earlier, studies have been carried out comparing the relative effectiveness of material and nonmaterial reinforcements with children of different socioeconomic backgrounds.[11] The results of these studies have been consistent: middle-class children responded as well to symbolic rewards as they did to material rewards such as candy or money. The performance of lower-class children, however, showed a marked decline when material rewards were absent.

Such research raises some serious questions. If lower-class children really are indifferent to classroom activities, as has been

---

9. P. T. Young and E. H. Shuford, Jr., "Quantitative Control of Motivation Through Sucrose Solutions of Different Concentrations," *Journal of Comparative and Physiological Psychology* (April 1955), pp. 114–18.
10. I. K. Waterhouse and I. L. Child, "Frustration and the Quality of Performance," *Journal of Personality* (March 1953), pp. 298–311.
11. E. Douvan, "Social Status and Success Striving," *Journal of Abnormal and Social Psychology* (March 1956), pp. 219–23; G. Terrell and W. A. Kennedy, "Discrimination Learning and Transposition in Children as a Function of the Nature of Reward," *Journal of Experimental Psychology* (April 1957), pp. 257–60; and G. Terrell, K. Durkin, and M. Wiesley, "Social Class and the Nature of the Incentive in Discrimination," *Journal of Abnormal and Social Psychology* (September 1959), pp. 270–72.

frequently stated, is this because there are fewer significant incentives for them in the typical school setting? How do we arrange reinforcements in a classroom where children come from various socioeconomic levels? Is the effectiveness of material rewards with lower-class children attributable to deprivation, or is it the result of learning within the lower-class culture? Socioeconomic class differences in preferences for incentives also suggest an explanation for the frequent difficulties encountered by middle-class teachers in trying to motivate lower-class children. Responding to symbolic reinforcements themselves, the teachers are confused and frustrated when students remain indifferent to such reinforcements.

Adopting a strict stimulus approach to the problems of motivation may free us from the need to deal with the problems of inaccessible and possibly nonexistent needs. But it leads to a number of other difficulties. To determine empirically the effectiveness of even a fraction of the possible reinforcers without recourse to some underlying theoretical framework presents a series of exceedingly complicated problems. The question, obviously, is never "Is this reinforcement effective?" but "Is it effective with this age or intelligence level? if applied on this schedule? with this socioeconomic class? with this task?" and so on through a great many other variables and combinations of variables, some of which are subtle and complex in their influence.

MOTIVATION: A RECONSIDERATION

The inaccessibility of needs is not the sole reason some psychologists prefer to emphasize stimulation rather than need reduction. Difficulties in applying a theory do not necessarily invalidate it, and drive reduction does provide a plausible, though complicated, account of many aspects of behavior, particularly in the areas of emotional and social behavior and personality development. However, at a number of points drive-reduction theory, at least in its conventional form, seems to contradict the facts.

A basic assumption of drive-reduction theory is that all behavior is motivated. This implies that organisms are inactive unless impelled into action in an effort to reduce the pain or discomfort associated with some unsatisfied homeostatic need or to avoid some stimulus that has been conditoned to a need. When it has not been possible to attribute a particular behavior to some already established need, psychologists have tended to posit new needs. The results of a number of experiments and informal observations contradict this view of organisms as inert until prodded into activity. Physiological research indicates that there is constant activity of the brain cells even during sleep, and a number of psychologists have reported play and exploratory behavior in young animals and children who were well fed and rested and who gave no indications of homeostatic need *or* strong environmental stimulation. Almost everyone has observed the persistence and enthusiasm with which happy, well-fed young children will repeat some newly acquired or emerging skill, such as walking, jumping, or manipulating some object. Intense stimulation, either external or arising from internal needs, tends to limit such behavior rather than to facilitate it.

To accept the view that activity is an intrinsic aspect of living organisms does not mean that we have to reject drive-reduction theory completely, with its implicit assumption that all activity is directed toward avoiding or eliminating stimulation. In fact, drive-reduction explanations fit some types of behavior very well. When stimulation becomes too intense—when noise rises above a bearable level, when hunger pangs become too strong, or when fatigue and anxiety mount—individuals develop techniques for reducing stimulation and satisfying needs. Moreover, these techniques often become well-established patterns of behavior that are resorted to each time similar conditions arise.

But the fact remains that there are some types of stimulation that we make no effort to avoid or eliminate, even though, in some cases, they are intense. The popularity of roller coasters, ghost stories, and horror movies among children and the lengths to which most adults will go to seek out exciting stimulation cast serious doubts on the general applicability of drive-reduction theory. The previously noted research on self-stimulation in animals with implanted electrodes also raises difficulties for a drive-reduction theory of motivation. What need does a rat reduce when he presses a bar in order to be stimulated through an electrode inserted in his brain? Is it possible to explain these exceptions without rejecting the concept of drive reduction entirely?

Some of the inadequacies of drive-reduction theory as an explanation for such behaviors may be overcome by introducing two additional ideas: *the possibility of two different types of stimulation, one innately positive, the other negative,* and *the concept of optimal levels of stimulation.*

Some forms of stimulation may be reinforcing at virtually all levels of intensity, and we make an effort to maintain or increase such stimulation, at least up to the point of satiation. On the other hand, stimulation arising from tissue damage is probably unpleasant at any perceptible level and arouses behavior aimed at eliminating it. Research on electrical stimulation of the brain appears to support the idea of innate positive and negative stimulation.[12] Direct electrical stimulation of the septal area seems to be positively reinforcing, while stimulation of portions of the brain stem is negatively reinforcing.

Most forms of stimulation, however, are apparently innately neither positive nor negative. Hebb has suggested[13] that when stimulation falls below a certain level, the organism becomes more active in an effort to increase the level of stimulation; when stimulation rises above this optimal level, the organism engages in behavior aimed at reducing its intensity. Above certain levels of intensity, these stimuli function in the same manner as innately negative stimuli. Below certain levels, they produce behavior similar to that aroused by innate positive stimulation. We avoid loud, shrill noises, for example, but we are restless and ill at ease in complete silence.

This theory of optimal levels of stimulation would offer an explanation for the discomfort of subjects in isolation experiments where stimulation of any sort is kept at a minimum. Anyone who has ever attempted to enforce a "rest period" in a nursery school or has required a group of first-graders to sit quietly with nothing to occupy their attention will recognize the possibilities in this explanation. This theory also offers an explanation for the decrease in exploratory and play activities when homeostatic needs or stimulation increase in intensity. Exploration and play decline because the child or young animal now engages in a narrower range of behavior aimed at reducing drive-induced or external stimulation to tolerable levels.

---

12. J. Olds and P. Milner, "Positive Reinforcement Produced by Electrical Stimulation of Septal Area and Other Regions of the Rat Brain," *Journal of Comparative and Physiological Psychology* (December 1954), pp. 419–27.
13. D. O. Hebb, "Drives and the Conceptual Nervous System," *Psychological Review,* Vol. LXII (1955), pp. 243–54.

What general conception of motivation remains after our consideration of these differing viewpoints? We can regard organisms, whether human or infrahuman, as being characterized by innate activity. The ancient Greek view that living matter is inert unless goaded into activity has dominated much of our thinking about motivation. It might be better to consider living things as intrinsically active energy systems upon which stimulation has a modifying rather than an initiating effect. Motivation may, then, be viewed as a process of directing and modulating activity rather than as a process of arousing the organism from inactivity.

This view of motivation is in a sense a hedonistic one, since it perceives the organism as attempting to maintain a pleasing state of affairs, not simply through the reduction of the discomfort associated with drives, but, in some instances, by maintaining stimulation within certain ranges of intensity and by seeking out some types of stimulation that are innately positive. It suggests, too, that, rather than considering ourselves handicapped because we cannot manipulate primary drives and make use of intense stimulation in motivating human beings, we should make an effort to avoid such extremes, since they tend to channel and restrict behavior. The inquisitive, exploratory behavior that we attempt to promote in learners seems most likely to occur in an environment that keeps them aroused without subjecting them to extremes of stimulation.

Suggestions for Class Discussion and Further Investigation

1. Do you agree with the statement that all learning results from some disturbance in the learner? Suppose one learns to enjoy Bach fugues; what kind of disturbance is involved?
2. What is meant by the statement that most rewards and punishments in human life are not innately rewarding or punishing but acquire these characteristics through learning?
3. Behavior arising from frustration has been described as "behavior without a goal." Do you agree with this description? Is a temper tantrum an example of respondent or instrumental behavior?
4. Paying people on a salary basis corresponds to what type of partial-reinforcement schedule? How do you account for the fact that all individuals receiving the same salaries do not perform at the same levels?

5. Do you think such reinforcers as praise, knowledge of results, or reduction of anxiety follow the principle of optimal levels of stimulation? What implications do you see in your answer for using these reinforcers in the classroom?
6. Is there *an* optimal level for any given form of stimulation, or does this level vary according to the maturity of the individual? What evidence do you have to support your opinion?
7. What are some physiological needs with which a teacher might occasionally be concerned in the classroom?

Suggestions for Further Reading

Two good general texts on motivation are J. S. Brown, *The Motivation of Behavior* (New York: McGraw-Hill, 1961); and J. F. Hall, *Psychology of Motivation* (Philadelphia: Lippincott, 1961).

For excellent summaries and comparisons of the various theories of motivation, see K. B. Madson, *Theories of Motivation* (Cleveland, Ohio: Howard Allen, 1961).

The "Nebraska Symposia on Motivation," published annually by the University of Nebraska Press, present a wide variety of articles on motivation by distinguished psychologists.

Some of the research mentioned in this chapter is discussed at length in articles by Harlow, Terrell, Wittrock, Bostrum, and Waterhouse and Child in Chapter 2 of J. P. DeCecco, *Human Learning in the School* (New York: Holt, Rinehart and Winston, 1963).

R. D. Archambault discusses the relationship of the concept of need to education in his article "The Concept of Need and Its Relation to Certain Aspects of Educational Theory," *Harvard Educational Review,* Vol. XXVII (1957), pp. 38–62.

Chapter Four

Motivation and Learning

Few conscientious teachers are completely satisfied with their ability to solve the motivational problems they encounter in their classrooms. Fewer still are satisfied with the recommendations for motivation that they encounter in the professional literature of education. Some of this dissatisfaction arises because of contradictions among the various recommendations. It may also arise from the common failure of both teachers and those who train teachers to distinguish between learning and performance.

Teachers are repeatedly told by presumed experts that if the material they present and their mode of presenting it to their students are interesting and "challenging," they will have no motivational problems. Children will learn readily and willingly with no special motivational efforts on the teacher's part. The reasonably intelligent teacher, however, soon becomes aware of the flaws in this argument: (1) the stimulating effect of any material and of any teaching procedure is at least partially determined by the needs and previous experiences of the learner; (2) most of the teaching techniques advocated as utilizing "intrinsic motivation" and "positive incentives" involve an appreciable element of coercion; (3) much of what must be taught to students is not, for various reasons, inherently interesting to them, and no amount of skill in presenting it is likely to make it so.

Some subjects, of course, seem to be intrinsically interesting to a *majority* of children; most young children in our culture want to learn to read and write, for example. But not all of them do, and only the most naive teacher would expect all pupils in a class to respond in the same way to the same subject or to the same mode of presentation. Children who come from homes where their parents read to them have already discovered that reading is a way of entering the fascinating world that exists between the covers of books. Others have yet to make this discovery; some never do.

Although we advocate grades, honor rolls, and other indications of adult approval as "positive incentives," there is nearly always at least an implied threat of failure and punishment for the individual who does not achieve or who does not respond appropriately. Skinner has pointed out that, while we have abandoned the birch rod, our means of controlling students remains essentially aversive; students now learn to avoid psychological punishment rather than physical punishment.[1] He has suggested that immediate knowledge of results is a much more desirable form of incentive than escape from punishment, particularly when the learning task is broken down into small steps and the knowledge is knowledge of success rather than of failure or error. There still remains the question, however, of whether such successes are important to the majority of students. Coleman's study, *The Adolescent Society*,[2] suggests that the really important systems of rewards and punishments in most secondary schools have little to do with academic achievement. The important rewards are those related to status in one's peer group, and status is largely determined by such factors as athletic participation, "rating-and-dating," cars, and spending money, rather than by academic success.

MOTIVATION AND PERFORMANCE

Most of the prescriptions for motivating students that are offered to teachers involve some form of external stimulation. Students, presumably, are impelled into learning something in order to attain status, win approval, avoid disapproval, or receive some more tangible reward. Admittedly, these procedures have not met with unqualified success. But if these procedures are not consistently effective, what justification exists for suggesting, as Skinner and other psychologists have, that extremes of stimulation be avoided in attempting to motivate students? Why not increase the intensity of stimulation?

To answer these questions, we must return to a distinction that

1. B. F. Skinner, "The Science of Learning and the Art of Teaching," *Harvard Educational Review*, Vol. XXIV (1954), pp. 86–97.
2. J. S. Coleman, *The Adolescent Society* (New York: Free Press of Glencoe), 1961.

has already been made: the distinction between performance and learning. Motivation directly affects performance but only *indirectly* affects learning, since learning apparently can occur through the contiguous association of stimuli, quite apart from motivation. To return to an earlier example—we need not assume that the child who has learned to fear the dark was motivated to do so.

Most motivational techniques are aimed at raising levels of performance, and, while what keeps the individual performing may also keep him learning, this is not inevitably so. As Deese has pointed out,[3] if an individual performs a particular act it is highly probable that this is because (1) he has learned to do so—that is, a particular response habit has been formed—and (2) because he is motivated to do so. Reinforcement, the essential element in motivational techniques, does not strengthen the habit so much as it provides an incentive for its use.

The relationships of performance to learning and of motivation to both performance and learning are complex and often obscure. Since we learn only what we experience, low levels of activity may result in low levels of learning because the learner is not sufficiently active to be exposed to the stimulation necessary if further learning is to occur. He makes too few trials or fails to try enough different approaches. However, as most teachers have observed, although intense stimulation (for example, high levels of anxiety) may result in a great deal of activity, it may be activity that is aimed at reducing the stimulation rather than at learning. Students may spend much of their time thumbing through notes, talking, or feverishly and unthinkingly underlining sentences in their texts. The central problem of motivation as it relates to *learning* requires securing the learner's attention and prompting him *to attend to the appropriate stimuli.* Very high levels of motivation may restrict the range of stimuli to which he attends and may possibly result in his attending to inappropriate stimuli. The point is that teachers should not assume that high levels of performance are synonymous with high levels of learning, nor should they assume that procedures resulting in greater student activity automatically result in greater learning. Quiet contemplation, reading for pleasure, browsing in the library, and similar activities may be as-

3. James Deese, *The Psychology of Learning,* 2nd ed. (New York: McGraw-Hill, 1958), p. 103.

sociated with low levels of motivation, but they may result in a great deal of worthwhile learning.

During our waking hours, and to a lesser extent while we are sleeping, we are continually attending to some stimuli and rejecting others. How to arouse students so that they attend to stimuli is obviously not the real problem in motivation; every individual is constantly attending to stimuli. The teacher's basic problem in motivating students is to find some means of causing them to respond to certain stimuli rather than to others, of focusing their attention on critical features in the learning task. It is simple to state the problem but difficult to solve it. Some of the stimuli to which we respond arise in the environment; others, including our own thoughts, arise internally. Some forms of stimulation seem to be innately attractive or repellent; others acquire these qualities as a result of our experiences with them. Moreover, our receptiveness to competing stimuli varies from time to time. When we are hungry the odor of food may capture our attention; we may ignore it when we are satiated or ill. Some forms of stimulation may override others; we may find it difficult to read during a radio commercial but have no difficulty in reading while music is being played.

As Bugelski has suggested,[4] motivational questions are essentially questions about factors affecting the relationship between stimulus and response. If, for example, a teacher presents a group of students with a task, they will probably respond in a variety of ways. Some will respond with enthusiasm, others with indifference or rebellion. The responses of some students to the task will be altered as a result of the teacher's manner, the activities of their classmates, or their own thoughts. At different times the same student may respond to the same task in different ways.

It is apparent that there are many conditions that can affect stimulus-response relationships, frequently in a very complicated manner. It is also apparent that no teacher can be constantly aware of all of these conditions. The teacher cannot know students' thresholds for different types of stimulation at any given moment. Nor can he hope to know all the previous experiences that might affect students' reactions to these stimuli or to competing stimuli.

---

4. B. R. Bugelski, *The Psychology of Learning* (New York: Holt, Rinehart and Winston, 1956), p. 241.

There are, of course, some forms of stimulation to which human beings respond rather consistently, and teachers can manipulate some stimulus conditions so as to affect the focus of students' attention. Sometimes complicated problems can be dealt with by relatively simple techniques, but there is always the danger that the simple solution does not take into consideration all the complexities of the problem. Bugelski has pointed out, somewhat facetiously, that since the teacher's primary motivational function is to get students to pay attention, "Sometimes even screaming at the children to *Pay attention!* may work." [5] But he also notes that we may solve the problem of attention in this way only to create a number of other problems.

EMOTIONS AS MOTIVES

We can scarcely imagine teachers using hunger, thirst, or electric shock to get students to pay attention. However, it is not uncommon for teachers to make students fearful and anxious in their efforts to motivate them. The threat of punishment, a hint that the teacher may talk with a parent or may increase the amount of homework, or the announcement of a test are all capable of raising the anxiety levels of students. Many teachers use such techniques so frequently and so efficiently that some adults, long after their school years, remain tense and anxious in the presence of a teacher.

The need to reduce anxiety differs from most other needs in one important respect: it is much more accessible to direct arousal and manipulation. In the normal course of human relations we are rarely able to make other people hungry or thirsty. We may be able to stimulate needs for affection or achievement, but it is likely to be a lengthy and uncertain process. It is relatively simple, however, to make people anxious and thus to arouse the need to reduce anxiety. Because this need is so much more accessible than other needs, anxiety arousal is likely to be frequently used as a technique for motivating students. What are the consequences of motivating students in this way? And, fundamental to this question, how do emotions, such as anxiety, function as motives?

Most psychologists have maintained that fears originate in trau-

5. *Ibid.*, p. 461.

matic experiences of helplessness in painful or unpleasant situations. Fears, according to this view, follow the paradigm of classical conditioning—that is, stimuli associated with traumatic experiences become conditioned stimuli for feelings of fear and anxiety. Presumably, then, the development of fear and anxiety requires some traumatic experience.

Some psychologists, however, have considered the possibility that some fears may arise in a very different fashion. Hebb noticed that young chimpanzees showed no signs of fear until they were approximately four months old, at which point familiar objects *in an unfamiliar guise* began to provoke withdrawal reactions and other indications of fear.[6] These feared objects were keepers or experimenters in strange clothes or in Halloween masks, strangers in the laboratory, a plaster cast of a chimpanzee's head, or a limp, anesthetized infant chimpanzee. These fear responses were immediate—that is, they were made to the initial encounter with the stranger, the detached head, or other fear-evoking stimulus and, therefore, could not be explained as the result of previous traumatic experience with these stimuli. However, stimulus objects with which the chimpanzees were completely unfamiliar did not elicit fear responses, and chimpanzees that had been repeatedly exposed to strangers showed no fear of newcomers. Completely familiar or completely unfamiliar stimuli apparently did not arouse fear in these animals, while familiar stimuli that had been changed in some manner frightened them even though these stimuli had not been previously associated with any traumatic experiences.

Other observers have noted that boys are less fearful in situations where physical risks are involved than are girls, despite the fact that boys commonly have more painful experiences in such situations than do girls.[7] Psychologists have also reported that rats that had been shocked and handled daily from birth until their twentieth day showed less emotionality in strange situations, despite their traumatic experiences, than did rats that had been left in the nest for the same length of time.[8]

6. D. O. Hebb, "On the Nature of Fear," *Psychological Review* (September 1946), pp. 259–76.
7. Frances B. Holmes, "An Experimental Study of the Fears of Young Children," in A. T. Jersild and F. B. Holmes, eds., *Children's Fears,* Child Development Monograph, Vol. XX (1953), pp. 167–296.
8. S. Levine, J. A. Chevalier, and S. J. Korchin, "The Effects of Shock and Handling on Later Avoidance Learning," *Journal of Personality* (June 1956), 475–93.

We have, then, data that run counter to the theory that fears arise out of traumatic experiences. We see young chimpanzees reacting with signs of fear to stimuli that have never been associated with pain, and we find children and young rats that have been subjected to traumatic experiences showing fewer signs of fear than those that have never been exposed to such experiences.

Hebb's interpretation of these findings,[9] essentially a physiological explanation, is that experience results in establishing certain patterns of neural activity in the brain. Experiences are stored as reverberating cerebral circuits, which he terms *cell assemblies.* A completely familiar stimulus activates one of these established patterns; a completely unfamiliar stimulus excites an entirely new cell assembly, of course. But a partially familiar stimulus, a familiar person in unfamiliar clothes, gives rise to excitation that is incongruous with an established pattern or cell assembly. This disrupts the organization of this pattern and, according to Hebb, is experienced as unpleasant emotion.

Whether or not we choose to accept this *incongruity-dissonance* explanation, as it has been termed, it seems evident that, although some fears unquestionably result from traumatic experiences, fears do not *always* have such an origin. Hebb's suggestion that some fears result from inadequate experience is compatible with the observed timidity and fearfulness of children whose experiences with adults have been pleasant but limited to their own family. We also note that most people enjoy talking with other individuals, but speaking before even a small audience is sufficiently different to be traumatic.

Given the existence of fears and anxieties, whatever their origins, how do they function as motives? Fear and anxiety, particularly at high levels of intensity, give rise to sensations that are very unpleasant and that the individual attempts to eliminate or reduce. Thus, anxiety, whether attributed to Hebb's incongruity-dissonance principle or explained on the basis of classical conditioning, leads to instrumental learning. One may not be able to exercise direct control over conditioned emotional reactions to fear-provoking stimuli, but one can learn ways to avoid situations that are anxiety provoking and attempt to reduce anxiety when it is aroused. Anxiety reduction, then, serves as a reinforcement for these behaviors.

---

9. Hebb, *op. cit.*

Attempts to reduce anxiety may produce behavior that is puzzling or annoying to others. The child who has acquired a fear of arithmetic may reject offers of assistance and continue making the same mistakes. To the teacher this behavior may appear stupid or downright perverse, but it is understandable if one recognizes that the child may be more intent on reducing his anxiety level by getting rid of a hovering teacher than on learning arithmetic. Other children may attempt to cope with anxiety by writing numbers down at random or, at the college level, by avoiding elective courses in subjects that evoke anxiety.

There are, of course, more constructive ways to deal with anxiety, and under some circumstances anxiety reduction can lead to increased learning. A number of studies have revealed that anxious students condition more readily in experimental situations. Bugelski contends that

> . . . it is pretty generally presumed that attention results when students are made or *become anxious.* How this comes about is not explained by currently prominent learning theorists. No other proposition has been advanced as the "drive" behind ordinary human learning. "Curiosity" itself is based on anxiety, according to Dollard and Miller (1950). The task of the teacher is to create the necessary degree of anxiety. The proposition that anxiety is the basic drive for human learning may appear paradoxical when teachers note that failures in arithmetic are so frequently associated with anxiety. The paradox is easily resolved in theory if we go on and demand that the anxiety must also be relieved at the conclusion of the correct response.[10]

Much has been made in recent years of curiosity as a basis for learning, particularly among human beings and primates. There is little question that much of our learning results from our inquisitive, exploratory behavior in new situations or when we are confronted with unfamiliar objects or events. If we accept Bugelski's viewpoint, it is unnecessary to postulate a separate "curiosity drive." Anxiety provoked by the unfamiliar is sufficient to explain such behavior. The teacher's role in instruction calls for arousing moderate levels of anxiety in students by making them aware of their state of "not knowing."

Research on inductive versus deductive approaches to learning has indicated that students who were encouraged to discover prin-

---

10. *Ibid.*, p. 461.

ciples for themselves tended to be more highly motivated and persistent in problem-solving situations than those who were given a principle they could apply. Frequently, those students who succeeded in learning inductively were able to use a principle in new situations, even though they could not express that principle in words with any precision. The situation continued to be much more open ended for them than for the group who had been given a definite rule. Conceivably, the lack of a definite, teacher-approved rule made the former group mildly anxious—and thus motivated.

We should note, however, that the relatively mild, task-oriented anxiety aroused by a state of not knowing may produce quite different results from the high levels of anxiety associated with punishment or threats of punishment. Observations of the performance of very anxious individuals suggest that such statements as "I was frightened out of my wits" may not be far from the truth. Although a mild degree of anxiety may produce alertness and attention, very high levels of anxiety may narrow the individual's range of perception and produce rigid, stereotyped behavior. Studies have shown that anxious students may perform well on simple, routine tasks, but their performance is likely to be poor on complex tasks requiring a flexible approach and the ability to perceive alternatives. Recent research, however, indicates that some highly anxious individuals may actually perform better on learning tasks under stress-provoking circumstances, *provided the stress can be reduced by learning.*

PUNISHMENT AND MOTIVATION

Punishment and the threat of punishment, although they may produce high levels of anxiety in the individual being punished and perhaps feelings of guilt on the part of the punisher, are very frequently used as a means of controlling behavior. How effective is punishment as a motivational technique? Is it a desirable procedure?

Most parents and teachers, although they may have some misgivings about the ethical aspects of punishing children, have strong suspicions, based on their own experiences, that punishment *is* effective in changing behavior. Most psychologists, however, stress the undesirable emotional effects of punishment and argue that punishment is not really a *motivational* procedure at all. Punishment, they contend, is the application of some noxious stimulus to behavior that is already at least reasonably well motivated. Punishment, from this point of view, is a procedure aimed at extinguishing behavior rather than a means of arousing behavior. Furthermore, they maintain that it is not effective even in this, since it usually produces only a temporary suppression of the punished behavior.

Punishment is, for most people, an emotionally loaded topic, and psychologists are not immune to the effects of emotion even when working within their own field of competency. Most of us feel that it is "wrong" to inflict pain unnecessarily or to control the behavior of a fellow being by force or the threat of force. Possibly for these reasons, the effects of punishment on behavior, particularly human behavior, have received less attention than have other areas of motivation, and some of the conclusions concerning punishment have been grossly oversimplified. Much of the professional literature even manages to avoid using the term, preferring to speak of "active avoidance learning" and "passive avoidance learning."

By *active avoidance learning,* psychologists mean a situation in which a subject can learn to avoid a painful or unpleasant stimulus by *doing* something—by escaping from a charged grid, jumping a hurdle to avoid a shock, or, conceivably, doing homework to avoid the teacher's displeasure. *Passive avoidance learning* is perhaps closer to what most of us have in mind when we think of learning resulting from punishment: by refraining from some act, by *not* doing something, we escape some unpleasant consequences. The hungry laboratory animal that refuses to eat from an electrically charged feeding dish and the angry child who restrains himself from striking a classmate in the teacher's presence are examples of passive avoidance learning.

Psychologists have tended to concentrate their attention on active-avoidance-learning experiments, and some contend that active and passive avoidance learning are fundamentally different processes. However, Solomon has suggested that, while in one case the subject is learning *what to do* and in the second case *what not to do,* the processes are essentially the same.[11] In both cases the individual is learning to avoid some noxious stimulus, and fear

11. R. L. Solomon, "Punishment," *American Psychologist* (April 1964), pp. 239–53.

responses are being conditioned to other stimuli in the situation. In both active and passive avoidance learning some operant response that differs from the punished behavior is being reinforced.

Research data appear to offer conflicting evidence on the effectiveness of punishment as a means of controlling behavior. One widely quoted study by Estes[12] indicated that punishing rats by shocking them when they pressed a bar to obtain food produced a temporary suppression but that the punished response ultimately returned to full strength. On the other hand, puppies that were punished by being slapped with a rolled newspaper for eating horsemeat would starve rather than eat when only horsemeat was available.[13] Similar results have been produced by shocking or frightening cats and monkeys during the act of eating.[14]

Solomon has suggested that differences in the effects of punishment may be partly a function of the particular point in a behavioral sequence at which the punishment occurs. If, for example, we shock a hungry animal and then release him from a box so that he may eat, his eating behavior may be unaffected by the shock. Indeed, he may come to act as though the shock were a signal that food is available. If we release him and punish him while he is trying to obtain the food, the same level of shock may stop his eating behavior, although the effect may be temporary. However, if we shock him while he is in the act of eating, we may disrupt this behavior permanently, and the animal may starve. Solomon insists that in considering the effects of punishment we must distinguish between instrumental acts and consummatory acts. Responses aimed at altering the environment or obtaining something from it are *instrumental acts.* Eating, drinking, or sexual behavior are examples of *consummatory acts.*

Events that precede, follow, or accompany punishment have an important effect upon reactions to the punishment, perhaps because they determine the interpretation the animal or the human being places upon the painful stimulation. The slap on the back following a friendly interchange does not produce the same reaction as the same blow from someone with whom we have been

12. W. K. Estes, "Experimental Studies of Punishment," *Psychological Monograph,* Vol. LVII, No. 3 (1944).
13. Solomon, *op. cit.*
14. J. H. Masserman, *Behavior and Neurosis* (Chicago: University of Chicago Press, 1943), pp. 66–90.

quarreling. If we are to avoid fallacious oversimplifications about the effects of punishment, it is apparent that we cannot consider punishment as an isolated event.

It is not safe to lump all types of behavior together in making assumptions about the effects of punishment. Experimental evidence [15] indicates that the effects of punishment depend upon the particular type of behavior being punished: (1) *behavior previously established by reward;* (2) *responses previously established by punishment;* (3) *complex innate responses*—that is, instinctual behavior; and (4) *discrete reflexes,* such as knee jerks or eye blinks.

The results of punishment on *instrumental acts* established by *positive reinforcement* are affected by a number of variables:

1. *The intensity of the punishment.* A very mild shock, for example, can serve as a cue and arouse or even intensify a response, while intense punishment may produce temporary, partial, or complete suppression of a response.

2. *Proximity, temporal or spatial, of the punishment to the response.* In general, punishment that immediately follows a response is more effective in extinguishing or suppressing the response than delayed punishment, and punishment that is administered in the vicinity where the behavior occurs tends to be more effective than punishment occurring in another location.

3. *The strength of the response.* Behavior that is well established —that is, behavior that is resistant to extinction after positive reinforcement has been withdrawn—will, ordinarily, be resistant to the effects of punishment.

4. *Adaptation to punishment.* Punishment introduced at a high level of intensity tends to be more effective than punishment that is slowly increased in intensity. New punishers are more effective than old punishers.

5. *The availability of nonpunished or rewarded alternative responses.* This variable is of particular importance in influencing the results of punishment. If we punish an instrumental response and permit no unpunished alternative, even intense punishment frequently produces only temporary or partial suppression of the punished behavior. If, however, an alternative response, a new means to the same end, is available, punishment of very low intensity can produce long-lasting suppression effects. The puppies

15. Solomon, *op. cit.*

that had been punished for eating horsemeat were permitted to eat pellets without being punished. Although being swatted with a newspaper was relatively mild punishment, they preferred to starve if only the prohibited horsemeat were available. Solomon has observed, "There is a valuable lesson here in the effective use of punishments in producing *impulse control. A rewarded alternative,* under discriminative control, makes passive avoidance training a potent behavioral influence. It can produce a highly reliable dog or child."[16]

What happens when we punish an active avoidance response—that is, a response that has been established by punishment? Punishing a child for being shy by criticizing and ridiculing him may, if the shyness is the result of previous criticism and ridicule, produce only further withdrawal. Using a different form of punishment may be somewhat more effective than employing the same punishment, but punishing responses that have previously been established by punishment is likely to intensify rather than eliminate them.

The effects of punishment on consummatory, as opposed to instrumental, behavior have not been thoroughly investigated. Two important differences do seem apparent, however. First, punishment seems to be particularly effective in disrupting consummatory behavior. Second, there is some indication that emotional responses, including neurotic disturbances, may be more severe when consummatory behavior is punished. Experiments with monkeys, dogs, cats, and rats have shown that the emotional consequences of punishing consummatory behavior may be devastating; among them are rigidity, regressions, displacement, aggressive behavior, and the development of ulcers. Masserman, using a toy snake to frighten monkeys while they were feeding, observed not only feeding inhibitions but unusual sexual behavior, prolonged periods of crying, and tics.[17]

Punishment does not *always* produce emotional disturbances, however. Under some circumstances punishment can be used effectively to change behavior with a minimum of emotional disturbance. Punishment seems to be most effective and to produce the fewest undesirable side effects if we apply it to instrumental rather than to consummatory behavior—that is, if we apply it when the individual is striving for but has not yet attained some goal,

---

16. *Ibid.,* p. 241.
17. Masserman, *op. cit.*

if there is some other response that will result in reinforcement, and if the unpunished alternative response is not too difficult to make.

We have considered the role of punishment in some detail for several reasons. First, punishment is widely employed in attempting to control behavior, and there seems little doubt that it can, *under some circumstances,* produce serious emotional side effects. Second, it is an area in which psychological opinion has been at variance with the opinions and experiences of nonpsychologists. Paradoxically, at the same time that psychologists have argued that punishment is a poor controller of instrumental behavior, some of them have also contended that it has a potent influence upon emotional behavior and may produce serious neurotic disturbances. Finally, a study of punishment illustrates the frequently complex nature of apparently simple problems.

It is now apparent that in order to answer our two original questions—How effective is punishment as a motivational technique? Is it a desirable technique?—we must first answer many other questions: What kind of behavior are we attempting to change? At what point in the behavioral sequence are we introducing punishment? What is the form of punishment? How intense is it? Is it a novel punishment or one to which the organism has perhaps become habituated?

Most of the research on punishment, for rather obvious reasons, has been carried on with animals, and the punishment has usually been some physical trauma, such as electric shock. In reactions to punishment there are species differences and probably maturational differences within species, and we cannot be sure that a child's reactions to punishment are the same as the reactions of a puppy or, for that matter, of an adolescent or an adult. Furthermore, the type of punishment employed with human beings is often symbolic rather than physical. A harsh word or an expression of distaste may be as punishing to a human being as a blow or an electric shock. We are likely to consider anxiety as one of the consequences of punishment; but anxiety itself, aroused perhaps by a word or a phrase, can be acutely punishing. Finally, in laboratory experiments on punishment we are usually able to predict the learner's behavior and punish him while he is attempting to attain some goal or at the moment he attains it. Much of the punishment meted out to human beings in nonlaboratory situations comes after the punished behavior has already been reinforced: a child takes a piece of cake, eats it, and is later spanked; or a pupil plays hooky, goes to the circus, and is punished when he returns to school.

Clearly, we must be cautious in making direct applications from the laboratory to the classroom or home. But the results of research on punishment should raise serious questions about some of our well-established practices. Ordinarily, for example, in attempting to eliminate some undesirable behavior, we start in with relatively mild punishment and increase its intensity until the behavior ceases. Laboratory data suggest that this is an inefficient procedure and may finally require punishment of much greater severity than would have been required initially to stop the behavior. Experimental evidence also suggests that a particular form of punishment, if used repeatedly, gradually loses its effectiveness as individuals adapt to it. This is evident in the case of the child who comes to ignore chronic scolding. We should also question the practice of "catching them in the act." If the particular act is an instance of consummatory behavior—eating, drinking, or sex play—we might predict, on the basis of laboratory research with animals as well as the reports of therapists, not simply a cessation of the behavior but the possibility of some truly horrendous side effects. And what may be the end results when parents punish a child and then, overcome with guilt, immediately comfort and reward him? Here we do not even have laboratory data to assist us, but our general knowledge of conditioning suggests the possibility that a pairing of pain and pleasure in this manner may result in masochistic tendencies.

In contrast to these dangerous or potentially dangerous aspects of punishment, we have Solomon's description of a rat that has been punished for incorrect responses and rewarded for correct ones: " . . . the rat, when the percentage of correct responses is high, looks like a hungry, well-motivated, happy rat, eager to get from his cage to the experimenter's hand and thence to the start box." [18]

Children, we realize, are not rats; their behavior is usually more complex than maze running, and it is doubtful that they respond to punishment in exactly the same manner. But situations do arise

---

18. Solomon, *op. cit.*, p. 250.

in dealing with children in which it seems urgent to eliminate undesirable behavior quickly. Should we resort to punishment? There is no single, comprehensive answer. Punishment is an effective means of changing some types of behavior, although there are, of course, many forms and varying degrees of punishment. Like many other potent procedures, punishment presents certain hazards, and its effects on behavior are complicated. Recognition of these factors increases the complexity of our decisions about the use of punishment, but it should also enable us to make more intelligent decisions.

SOCIAL MOTIVATION

Much of our behavior appears to arise from so-called *social motives*. We attend parties, spend hours talking with friends, and compete with fellow students. We tolerate the noise and discomfort of crowds, eat when we are not hungry or eat things we do not like, and voluntarily submit to boring and occasionally painful social rituals because of our social expectations or the expectations of others.

Because we live and behave in an environment that requires almost constant interaction with others, almost all human behavior is affected in some manner by social experiences. Consequently, "social motivation" has tended to become a catchall category of explanations for a wide variety of human behaviors ranging from joining clubs and striving for status and success to attempting to understand one's self and one's environment. These behaviors are certainly real enough, and they occur frequently. But it is less certain that these behaviors arise from innate and universal needs for affiliation, achievement, dominance, or self-acceptance and self-understanding. The concepts of conditioning, operant learning, and secondary reinforcement offer a reasonable and more economical explanation. Most of us, for example, seem to be bothered by ambiguity and by inconsistencies and discrepancies in our own thinking. Festinger has developed an interesting theory of *cognitive dissonance* based on the hypothesis that human beings are strongly motivated to be logical and internally consistent in their thought processes.[19] When a person holds mutually contradictory or incon-

19. L. Festinger, *A Theory of Cognitive Dissonance* (Evanston, Ill.: Row, Peterson, 1957).

sistent ideas, a state of dissonance occurs; he is uncomfortable and makes an effort to achieve consistency and consonance. Although this theory is not restricted to social motivation, it has been applied to explain motivation in a wide variety of social situations. The person, for example, who has a negative attitude toward a minority group but is friendly toward an individual member of this group may be motivated by his feelings of dissonance to rationalize that this particular individual is "different" and not representative of his group. Efforts to be internally consistent are too readily observable for us to doubt the existence of such motivation. But its existence can be explained without assuming that all human beings have an innate need to be consistent. It is possible that such remarks as "You're contradicting yourself," "That's nonsense," or "Be logical about this" are part of the process whereby children are conditioned to avoid inconsistencies.

Two broad areas of social motivation that are of particular interest to educators are *attitude development* and *achievement motivation.*

Many of the variations in individual responses to incentives and to opportunities to achieve appear to be related to attitudinal learnings. Our behavior is affected by attitudes toward a wide variety of objects and events, toward other individuals, and toward ourselves. Children brought up in different environments frequently have markedly different attitudes toward teachers, competitive activities, school subjects, and scholastic achievement in general. To some children, each encounter with unfamiliar material or with a new situation is threatening, while others display a lively curiosity and an eagerness to investigate.

Attitudes have been defined as persistent, learned states of readiness to react in a consistent way toward some class of objects or events. The individual who has a negative attitude toward dogs, for example, reacts in much the same way to all dogs, although some dogs are gentle and friendly, while others are vicious or suspicious. The development of some attitudes seems to follow the paradigm of classical conditioning: traumatic experiences associated with dogs, mathematics, or some item of food can result in a conditioned response to these stimuli. Other attitudes appear to develop through operant learning: the individual finds that certain expressions of attitude are approved and supported by others.

On the basis of Festinger's cognitive-dissonance theory, we would expect individuals to find it difficult to maintain attitudes that are inconsistent with their own behavior or with other attitudes they hold. Conversely, the person who holds attitudes that are consistent with those of his parents, peers, or other individuals whom he respects is reinforced both by achieving consonance and by the support of others. One of the difficulties that teachers sometimes encounter in trying to change attitudes is this constant and sometimes subtle flow of reinforcement that prevents the extinction of existing attitudes.

Attitudes may directly affect learning by causing us to misperceive stimuli. If we perceive all teachers as ogres or mathematics as a form of torture, we respond inappropriately. Sometimes these inappropriate responses result in further reinforcement of our attitudes when teachers do become angry or our feelings about mathematics make it still more difficult to learn.

The expression "the achievement motive" tends to suggest that motivation to succeed can be explained in terms of some unitary motive or need. Since human beings exhibit such great variability in their drive for success, a reasonable assumption is that this is a derived rather than an innate motive—that it is the result of learning and secondary reinforcement. The fact that there are also rather well-defined social class and cultural differences in achievement motivation supports this viewpoint. Were we able to assume that individual social experiences were similar enough so that all or most of the students in our schools were motivated to achieve (an assumption we obviously cannot make), we would still have to reckon with the effects of individual experiences with success and failure.

Studies of the effects of competition on student motivation and studies of goal-setting behavior indicate that some individuals respond effectively and realistically in competitive situations, while others of equal ability are disorganized and discouraged by competition. For some students, competitive situations provoke relatively mild and manageable levels of anxiety, and their performance may be improved by the competition. Others, particularly those with past histories of lack of success may have developed negative attitudes toward their own competence. Not only may they be directly handicapped by the disruptive effects of high levels of anxiety on their thinking, but they may attempt to reduce their anxiety in ways that are detrimental to achievement. Some of these students may set unrealistically low goals, while others, in an "A-for-effort" attempt, may set their goals well beyond any reasonable hope of achievement. Some children may attempt to lower their anxiety level by convincing themselves that academic achievement is unimportant.

For the teacher, the problem of dealing with the effects of competition is a formidably complicated one. However, teachers' levels of aspiration and goal-setting behavior should be realistic, too. Teachers are subject to the usual limitations of human beings and should not expect to deal with all the problems of every student. Although children will always present serious motivational problems, in a society such as ours it is reasonable to assume that the majority of students have some desire to succeed. Motivational techniques that keep anxiety at moderate levels, that direct the student's attention to critical elements in the learning task, and that provide opportunities for adequate reinforcement will probably be successful with most students.

This is, of course, an overly simplified statement of the teacher's role in the motivation of learners, but it is not intended as a prescription for the teacher to follow or a description of teaching methods—nor is it meant to imply that the problem is a simple one. Motivation itself cannot be directly manipulated by the teacher; rather, it results *from* manipulation. "Motivation," as we have already noted, is a term applied to a number of conditions affecting stimulus-response relationships, and teachers *can* manipulate these conditions. Stimuli involved in reinforcement or anxiety arousal, for example, though not completely under the teacher's control, can be manipulated a great deal. *How* teachers should arrange the conditions of stimulation to promote learning is a complex problem. An understanding of the variables in motivation may not make the problem less complex, but it may provide a basis for formulating effective motivational techniques.

Suggestions for Class Discussion and Further Investigation

1. A frequent suggestion for motivating students is to give them a share in planning what they are to learn. Do you think this is desirable? Would you place any qualifications on your answer with respect to grade level, subject, or extent of pupil planning?
2. Many adults who complained and rebelled at practicing the

piano or some other musical instrument now wish their parents had insisted they continue their practice and their lessons. Should we coerce children into practicing?

3. It has been said that success is relative, that each individual adjusts his level of aspiration and judges his own performance in such a way as to insure a relatively constant percentage of successes. Do you believe this? Does this mean that we need not be concerned about the student who has a great many failures?
4. Competition is frequently used as a means of motivating students. Under what conditions is this desirable?
5. Why do we have no good research data on the effects of punishing an instrumental response *after* it has been reinforced?
6. Neurotic behavior has been defined as "persistent, nonadjustive behavior." If it is nonadjustive, why does it persist? Do you think such problems are learning problems?
7. Consider the attitudes some individuals hold toward members of minority groups. Are these attitudes motives or tendencies to respond in a particular manner to certain stimuli?
8. Young children characteristically are enthusiastic and spontaneous in their reactions to nearly all aspects of their environment. Much of this spontaneity and enthusiasm disappears after they have been in school for a few years. Have we stamped out spontaneity or simply made the children more discriminating in their reactions to their environment?
9. What would you expect to be the result of assigning additional schoolwork as a means of punishing students? Why do you suppose teachers do this? Why is arithmetic a favorite subject for such assignments?
10. Do you think students will work harder when attempting to achieve group goals or when working for themselves?

Suggestions for Further Reading

Personality differences complicate our efforts to understand human motivation. Dorothy Rethlingshafer provides useful information on this subject in her *Motivation as Related to Personality* (New York: McGraw-Hill, 1963). The chapter "Motivation and Learning" is of particular value to teachers.

Edward J. Murray, *Motivation and Emotion* (New York: Prentice-Hall, 1964) offers a concise (118-page) well-written discussion of motivation, with emphasis in Chapters 5, 7, and 8 on emotions and the role of social motives in behavior.

Teachers spend much time criticizing and correcting students' papers. The effectiveness of this procedure in improving students' performance is discussed in Ellis B. Page, "Teacher Comments and Student Performance: A Seventy-Four Classroom Experiment in School Motivation," *Journal of Educational Psychology* (August 1958), pp. 173–81.

The effects of another instructional procedure on motivation are examined in Bert Y. Kersh, "The Motivating Effect of Learning by Directed Discovery," *Journal of Educational Psychology* (April 1962), pp. 65–71.

Many of the educational goals that we ask students to work toward are far removed in time from their immediate classroom activities. John E. Teahan, "Future Time Perspective, Optimism, and Academic Achievement," *Journal of Abnormal and Social Psychology* (November 1958), pp. 379–80, considers some of the ways in which successful students may differ from unsuccessful ones in their responses to long-term goals.

The following articles are concerned with the role of group pressures in motivation: Solomon E. Asch, "Opinions and Social Pressures," *Scientific American* (November 1955), pp. 31–35; and Marvin E. Shaw, "Some Motivational Factors in Cooperation and Competition," *Journal of Personality* (June 1958), pp. 155–69.

The focus of educational psychology has been on the individual student, whereas the social psychologist has been concerned primarily with the group and with intragroup relations. Students do learn in groups; and W. C. Trow, A. F. Zander, W. C. Morse, and D. H. Jenkins, in their article "Psychology of Group Behavior: The Class as a Group," *Journal of Educational Psychology* (October 1950), pp. 322–38, have considered the effects upon learning of group-derived attitudes, cohesiveness of the group, group resistance to change, and the goals of the group.

Chapter Five

Verbal Behavior and Concept Formation

Language is undoubtedly man's most conspicuous achievement, an achievement that distinguishes him from all other forms of life. Because verbal behavior is so distinctively human, its study holds forth the promise of yielding unique insights into human behavior. It is true, of course, that what a person says can tell us a great deal about what he is thinking, planning, or wanting, but the study of man's verbal behavior also presents us with many additional problems and questions.

Man is obviously not born with the ability to use language. How does he acquire the ability to speak and to comprehend the speech of others? How do his language skills influence the way he perceives his environment? How does language affect his ability to solve problems, to learn nonverbal skills, or to retain what he has learned? Why do some individuals differ in their facility with language? Is there some relationship between language and emotional disorders?

Other problems centering around verbal behavior are of a somewhat different nature. Many psychologists contend that man's ability to deal with abstract ideas—to acquire concepts, for example—is dependent upon his ability to use language. Yet, we find people effectively employing concepts that they are unable to verbalize; and we observe monkeys, rats, and even chickens displaying behavior that suggests that they have acquired concepts of shape, size, or position. Is the ability to think abstractly dependent upon the ability to use language?

In studying the behavior of animals below the level of man, we are handicapped because we cannot ask an animal questions about his behavior; we can only draw inferences from what we observe. Yet, much of our difficulty in understanding human behavior stems from the fact that a great deal of it is verbally mediated—that is, between stimulus and final, overt response, certain internal events occur. A rat, for example, is essentially a sensing and reacting organism; when stimulated, he responds directly to the stimulus. A human being, on the other hand, when stimulated, may consider various possible responses, select from among these alternatives, decide on his line of action, and then respond. Rather than a single, observable response to the stimulus, he may make a series of verbal responses, each serving as a stimulus for other verbal responses. This chaining of stimulus-response-stimulus-response using verbal symbols need not result in any outward indications of what is going on within the individual. This internal, symbolic mediation of responses greatly complicates the study of human behavior in still another way: because human beings can use language to recapture past experiences and to anticipate future events, they are frequently responding to stimuli that are not physically present. Consequently, we are often surprised and perplexed by sudden twists and turns in human behavior.

LANGUAGE AS AN INTERVENING VARIABLE

Language can be viewed as a complex set of responses that the individual uses to communicate with and to influence others. Understanding this aspect of language is complicated enough, and scores of articles and books have been written on the subject. But language, as we have noted, also serves an *intra*communication function—that is, it is a means by which the individual can stimulate, direct, organize, and sometimes reinforce his own behavior. Through his ability to use language, man has acquired the capacity to bring his behavior under some degree of *internal* control.

Thought and *thinking* are the terms we customarily apply to these covert verbal responses to stimuli that are not immediately present in the environment, to this internal manipulation of symbols that represent sensations and perceptions. Not all thinking makes use of language, of course. The swimmer poised on the end of the board and planning a dive and the musician mentally "listening" to the music he is composing are probably not engaged in a completely linguistic form of thinking. It has been shown, too, that deaf children who apparently have not acquired language in the usual sense of the term can acquire concepts and can solve problems requiring them to compare sizes, forms, and colors and to remember associations. But there is little question that much of our thinking follows verbal patterns. By making available, in symbolic form, the results of previous experience, language can provide a series of cues that serve to direct subsequent behavior. In this manner, language can function as an intervening variable in learning, modifying our responses to external stimuli.

This ability to bring the past into the present and to anticipate the future, provides the human learner with some enormous advantages in learning. Language not only enhances our ability to profit from our own experiences; it enables us to use the experiences of others efficiently. Mowrer has observed, for example, that "one can do almost anything more easily if told how, than if one has to discover the solution independently or on the basis of one's own random (or even well-reasoned) exploratory efforts." [1] Language can also create problems for man. Our verbal symbols, because they can represent experiences, can also elicit many of the emotional responses associated with those experiences. Despite poetic references to "poor little frightened, hunted hares," it appears that animals below the level of man, once danger has passed, go about their affairs with little residual anxiety. Man, however, being capable of carrying his experiences with him symbolically, often finds his emotional responses being called forth by *internal verbal stimuli* rather than by external events. Long after some traumatic experience, a word or phrase may be sufficient to arouse the original anxiety reactions. The effects of our ability to acquire and use language pervade all aspects of our behavior, our emotional reactions as well as our cognitive responses.

LANGUAGE AS INSTRUMENTAL BEHAVIOR

Every individual (except those who are seriously retarded) learns the language of his society, usually at a relatively early age. We spend most of our waking hours in some form of verbal behavior—thinking, talking, and listening to others. But we have a limited understanding of the manner in which we acquire the ability to use language. There is considerable knowledge about language

1. O. H. Mowrer, *Learning Theory and Personality Dynamics* (New York: Ronald, 1950), p. 671.

development—the growth of children's ability to use language, the extent of their vocabularies at various ages, and the emergence of certain verbal patterns. But *how* do children learn to speak and to understand the speech of others? Those sounds that we call words are encountered by the child as *stimuli*; by what process does he learn to reproduce them as responses? How do words acquire *meaning*?

B. F. Skinner has considered language acquisition as another instance of instrumental learning and has analyzed it in terms of the behavioral functions it serves.[2] Such expressions as "Come here," "Tell me," or "Let's turn the page" are intended to produce some change in the environment. Skinner has labeled these expressions *mands*. "I wonder how to do this," "Have you noticed this picture?" and similar expressions serve to direct one's attention or the attention of others toward some aspect of the environment. These Skinner has termed *tacts*.

The learning of both mands and tacts, according to Skinner, follows the basic paradigm for operant responses: in the presence of some discriminative stimulus (a stimulus that the learner can discriminate or differentiate from the rest of his environment), a response is made and followed by a positive reinforcement. (See Figure 2.) In the learning of *mands,* the discriminative stimulus is most often some adult who reinforces the child's behavior, perhaps giving him a drink when he makes a verbal response that is recognizable, such as "water" or "drink," or by coming when the child calls. In learning *tacts*—learning to name objects, for example —if the child responds to some discriminative stimulus with an appropriate utterance, reinforcement usually follows in the form of adult approval. A small child saying something that sounds like "cow" when a cow is pointed out to him usually neither wants nor receives a cow, but his verbal efforts are likely to be praised by a proud parent.

This theory of language development relies heavily on reinforcement in explaining how verbal responses are acquired; but, as we have noted, not all psychologists agree that reinforcement is necessary for learning.

A second, less theoretical objection has been raised. Before a child can be reinforced for a successful verbal response, he must

---

2. B. F. Skinner, *Verbal Behavior* (New York: Appleton-Century-Crofts, 1957).

FIGURE 2

OPERANT PARADIGMS FOR LEARNING VERBAL RESPONSES

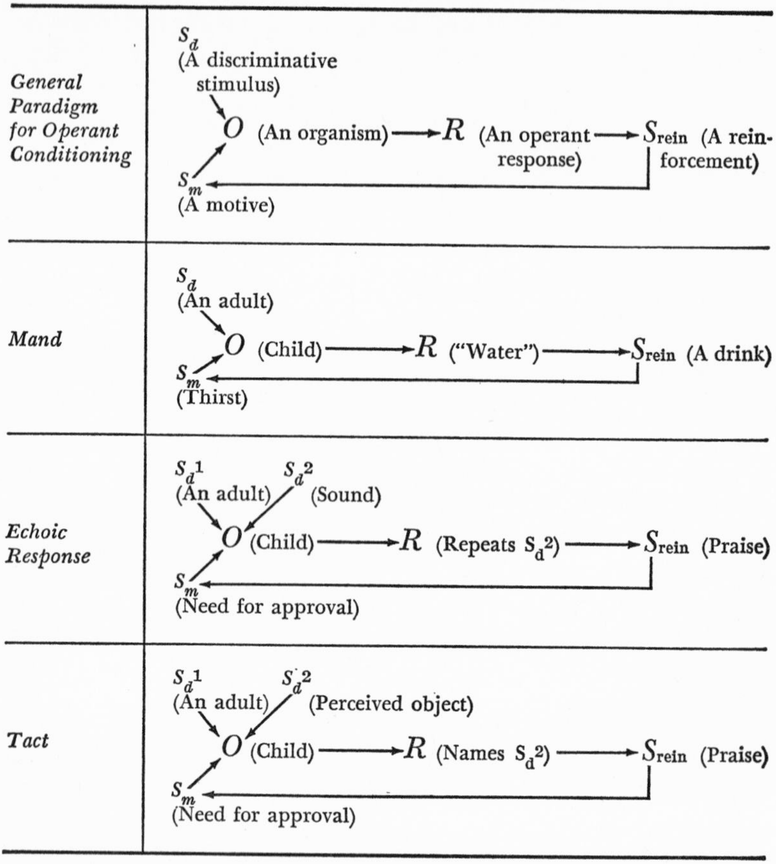

General Paradigm for Operant Conditioning	S_d (A discriminative stimulus) → O (An organism) → R (An operant response) → S_{rein} (A reinforcement) → S_m (A motive) → O
Mand	S_d (An adult) → O (Child) → R ("Water") → S_{rein} (A drink) → S_m (Thirst) → O
Echoic Response	S_d^1 (An adult) → O; S_d^2 (Sound) → O (Child) → R (Repeats S_d^2) → S_{rein} (Praise) → S_m (Need for approval) → O
Tact	S_d^1 (An adult) → O; S_d^2 (Perceived object) → O (Child) → R (Names S_d^2) → S_{rein} (Praise) → S_m (Need for approval) → O

first make such a response. Of all the possible sounds he might make, what is the probability that a child, in the presence of some stimulus object, will make a sound even approximately like the name of that object?

This problem of eliciting a correct or approximately correct initial response can be overcome if we first train the child to make echoic responses—to imitate sounds made by others. These echoic responses can then be linked to tacts or mands. John Whiting has suggested that adults may accomplish this unintentionally by imitating the infant's babbling while petting, praising, and smiling at him.[3] In this manner the young child associates social reinforcement with making the same sounds as those made by the adult. Once this association has been made, it is a simple matter to cause the child to echo the sound "drink" when there are indications that he is thirsty or to repeat after an adult the name of some stimulus. Similarly, the child can later be taught to make verbal responses to printed stimuli, linking these to mands, tacts, and other verbal responses.

THE ACQUISITION OF MEANING

A strictly operant approach to language, if it does not ignore the problem of meaning entirely, at least does not assign it a central role. It is probably true, as Lorge has pointed out, that "Language, for the child, is a way of behaving. It is not, initially, a mode for thought or for reflection." [4] Mowrer, too, has stressed the distinction between "words as used" and "words as understood," pointing out that while " 'mama' is the symbol used by adults (and older children) to refer to a particular person in the household," the young child probably first employs this word to indicate discomfort or to demand attention.[5] "Mama," as initially used by the child is a mand; he uses it to obtain something from his environment. Later he is able to use it as a tact—as a means of indicating some particular aspect of his environment.

In some way, a response that has been learned as a mand has come to be available to the child for use as a tact. Similarly, expressions learned as tacts can be used as mands without the child's going through the process of learning them as mands. A child who learns to name an object—a ball, for example—is immediately able to use this response to demand the ball when he wants it. Apparently, not only does the child learn to make verbal responses, but in some manner these responses acquire *meaning* for him.

Since speech is a motor response, the operant paradigm seems appropriate for explaining its acquisition. Nevertheless, speech

---

3. Cited by O. H. Mowrer in *op. cit.*, p. 686.
4. Irving Lorge, "How the Psychologist Views Communication," in John P. DeCecco, ed., *Human Learning in the Schools* (New York: Holt, Rinehart, and Winston, 1963), p. 333.
5. Mowrer, *op. cit.*, p. 674.

is only one aspect of language. The child also learns not only to make sounds but to respond to and to understand verbal stimuli. How does the individual learn the *meaning* of words?

In any operant learning situation, there are elements of classical conditioning. As Figure 3 indicates, the child who says "Water"

FIGURE 3

CLASSICAL CONDITIONING OF MEANING RESPONSES

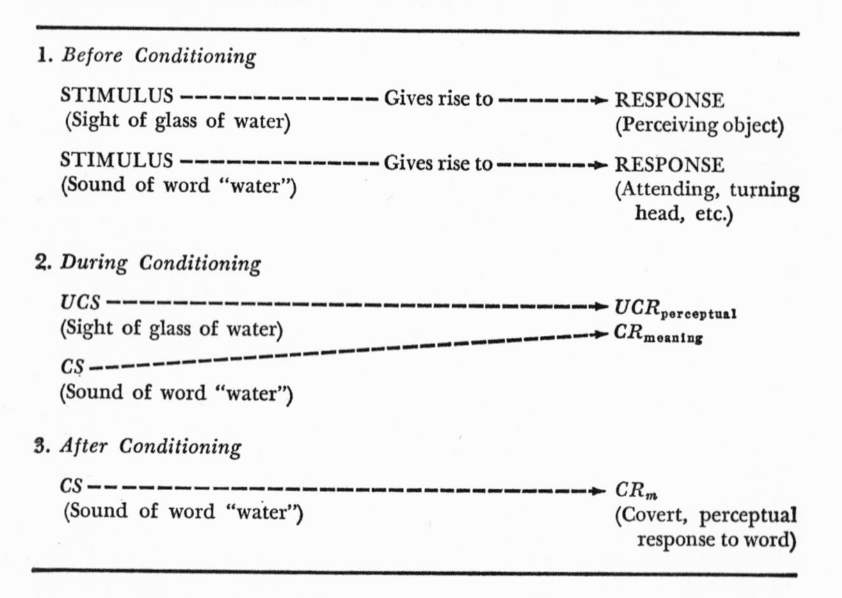

when he is thirsty is reinforced for this response by being given a glass of water. At the same time, the glass of water, an unconditioned stimulus, is paired with the sound "water." But for what response is the glass of water an unconditioned stimulus? The sight of a glass of water is obviously not an unconditioned stimulus for the verbal response "water"; this must be learned. However, stimuli such as glasses of water do produce covert, unconditioned perceptual responses in the same manner that any stimulus that impinges upon our receptors produces a response, even though the stimulus may not be familiar or one that we can identify or name. By consistent pairing of the *UCS* (in this case the sight of a glass of water) with the *CS* (the sound "water"), the *CS* comes to evoke a conditioned response (*CR*) that approximates the response previously evoked by the *UCS*. This conditioned response to the word "water" can be termed a *meaning response*.[6]

Whether this conditioning process accompanies the learning of either a mand or a tact is unimportant. Once the meaning response has been acquired, it can function in either of these contexts. This would account for the fact that a word learned as a tact can function as a mand and vice versa.

In the early stages of language development, the child learns a direct correspondence between words and objects ("Here's your *ball*"), words and events ("Mother is *coming*"), and words and qualities ("Careful! It's *hot!*") This direct correspondence is "meaning" for the young child, and it results from the combined effects of operant and classical conditioning.

This is a simplified view of meaning. As the child progresses beyond this "naming stage," we probably need to distinguish between *denotative* meaning and *connotative* meaning. The usual dictionary definitions of nouns are examples of denotative meanings. To learn the denotative meaning of "cat," the individual must learn which patterns or properties of stimulation are criterial in determining whether an animal is or is not a cat. But, in addition to its denotative meaning, "cat" has a connotative meaning; such abstract qualities as "aloof," "stealthy," or "independent" are suggested by this term. Though associated with "cat," they are noncriterial attributes and, so far as denotation is concerned, are irrelevant. As we noted in Chapter Two, there is evidence that connotative meanings can be classically conditioned (see p. 27).

With increased experience, the child learns that the meanings of words depend also upon the context or situation in which they occur. *Situational meaning* arises, in part, from the fact that words, as we use them in our language, follow one another on the basis of certain linguistic probabilities. The probability that a noun will follow an article is very high; the probability that one article will follow another is exceedingly low. There are also varying probabilities that certain words will occur together. The expression "pretty smile" occurs frequently, but "pretty meat" would strike us as most unusual. We would have difficulty in ascribing

6. For a more detailed discussion see J. B. Carroll, *Language and Thought* (New York: Prentice-Hall, 1964), pp. 38–40.

meaning to a group of words in which the words occurred in the following sequence. "Man forced depends circumstantially every intrusion," because we try to interpret the individual words in relationship to one another. We also find that the meanings of individual words change as we relate them to other words. "Pretty" means one thing when paired with "smile." It means something quite different when paired with "good."

We also learn, beginning at an early age, to respond to linguistic patterns. This is apparent from the grammatical errors children make. The child who says "throwed" rather than "threw" is indicating an awareness of the general pattern of adding *ed* to form the past tense. Roger Brown has reported that if *ing* is added to a nonsense syllable, it conveys a sense of action to children; prefacing a nonsense syllable with the word "some" leads children to interpret the nonsense syllable as a mass noun. He has concluded that at a very young age children learn classes of words—at least verbs and nouns and, possibly, adjectives.[7] Such learning adds another dimension of meaning to verbal stimuli.

Teachers and others who are concerned with verbal behavior have commented on both the persistence of early speech patterns and the difficulties of teaching a new language. Study of early verbal behavior suggests some reasons for both these problems. We learn the language of our own culture largely on an informal and incidental basis. Children are given some direct instruction by parents and other children, but much of their learning of grammatical constructions, proper accent, and appropriate choice of words is incidental to satisfying other needs. This contrasts sharply with the manner in which grammar and foreign languages are taught in our schools. A child learning to talk is highly motivated, because it is a means to important ends and because he is promptly reinforced for making appropriate verbal responses. Moreover, he gets tremendous amounts of practice. It is very difficult to reproduce these conditions in the classroom or the language laboratory, although efforts to do so have been made in some recent approaches to the teaching of grammar and the teaching of foreign languages.

---

7. Roger W. Brown, "Linguistic Determinism and the Part of Speech," *Journal of Abnormal and Social Psychology* (July 1957), pp. 1–5.

CONCEPT FORMATION

One reason we do not spend our entire lives in the "vast, blooming, buzzing confusion" that William James described as the world of the newborn infant is that we are able to acquire and use concepts. Concept formation is a critically important aspect of human learning. The acquisition of concepts serves to simplify an otherwise bewilderingly complex world and to provide us with a reasonably stable basis for perceiving and interpreting both our environment and our own behavior.

There are, for example, hundreds of thousands of teachers in our schools. They differ from one another in many ways—in appearance, temperament, intelligence, and attitudes. Yet they have certain attributes in common by which we can identify them as teachers. By classifying them as "teachers" we are able to simplify our task of learning appropriate responses to them. Similarly, in acquiring other concepts we organize our environment, eliminate some of its complexities, and reduce the dimensions of the learning tasks that confront us. This is true, of course, only if our concepts are both accurate and adequate. Children who conceive of all teachers as ogres and others who think of all dogs as friendly, playful animals are likely to make serious errors in their responses to teachers and dogs. Since the concepts we acquire so powerfully affect our perceptions, concept formation is of particular interest to those concerned with human learning.

The relationship of language to concept formation is neither simple nor straightforward. Language does facilitate our *use* of concepts and, as Skinner has pointed out, language assures that there will be a certain degree of uniformity among the concepts employed in communities sharing the same language.[8] However, we often find individuals employing the same verbal labels for what turn out to be quite different concepts.

Concept formation, moreover, involves more than simply learning to label some object or event. Each of us can apply the term "tree" appropriately. We can readily discriminate trees from telephone poles, bushes, flowers, and fire hydrants. If requested to draw a tree, most of us can produce something recognizable to others as a tree. But the tree we draw does not adequately illustrate our

8. Skinner, *op. cit.*, p. 8.

concept of a tree. No single drawing could, since towering redwoods, stunted and twisted pines, cocoanut palms, and apple trees are all recognized by us as trees. It is apparent that these stimulus events are not, in themselves, concepts and that when we speak of a concept we are referring not to a specific entity or even to a specific set of experiences but to *classifications* or *categories* of experience. The particular objects we categorize as trees may differ widely with respect to many characteristics, but they possess certain criterial attributes that determine our responses to them. Therefore, we place them in the same conceptual category.

Concept formation, then, involves *abstraction,* the discrimination of the criterial or definitive attributes of a concept. Especially in the early stages of learning a concept, the learner may fail to perceive these distinguishing characteristics or may concentrate on some and ignore others. Small children, for example, may call cats, rabbits, and toy bears "dog" or mistake trucks for cars. This tendency to respond to similar stimuli as though they were identical is termed *stimulus generalization.*

Concept formation may seem, at first thought, to be essentially a process of breaking down this tendency toward stimulus generalization. However, some degree of generalization is necessary if our categories of experience are to encompass more than single events. In acquiring the concept "man," we must discriminate men from women and from boys; but, at the same time, we generalize to the extent that tall men, short men, old men, and men with and without beards are all categorized as "men." Fundamentally, concept formation requires that we learn to make necessary discriminations, while avoiding inappropriate ones.

Some of our responses are undoubtedly learned on the basis of a single trial. Concept formation, however, calls for categorizing stimulus events having certain common characteristics. Consequently, more than a single experience is necessary. Continued and, particularly, varied experience results in changes and refinements in our concepts. In this sense, many of our concepts are probably never completely acquired. The average individual probably possesses what seems to him to be a perfectly adequate concept of reptiles; but, to the herpetologist, with his greater background of experience, such a concept is woefully inadequate. Experience also tends to increase the number of concepts we attain. Eskimos, for example, have different terms for different types of snow. Presumably their vocabulary reflects not only greater experience but the need for more precise ways of thinking about snow.

One of the critical problems for the teacher is to arrange, within the limits of available time and facilities, experiences that will facilitate the acquisition of adequate concepts, while avoiding the development of misconceptions. The latter usually result from conceptualizations based on nonexistent characteristics, such as the belief that snakes are slimy, or on irrelevant characteristics, such as skin color as a basis for social categories.

Concept-Formation Tasks. Not all concepts are learned with equal facility. In attempting to explain this, psychologists have considered both differences in the nature of concepts themselves and variations in the processes by which concepts are acquired. It has been suggested that considering concepts under three categories, conjunctive, disjunctive, and relational, may provide a clearer view of the problems confronted by the learner in concept formation.[9]

In the case of *conjunctive concepts,* all relevant attributes must be present. The absence of one of them places the object or event in a different category. The child learning the concept of "horse" finds that it is identified by having a mane and a tail, undivided hoofs, and certain eating habits, and being of a particular size and shape. If it has cleft hoofs, for example, it is not a horse.

Disjunctive concepts include two or more sets of characteristics that are usually mutually exclusive. A "down" in football, for example, may result from the ball carrier's being tackled, the throwing of an incomplete pass, or the ball carrier's being forced out of bounds. Disjunctive concepts often appear more difficult to learn than conjunctive concepts.

"Larger than," "to the north of," and "alike" are examples of *relational concepts.* Since their attributes are usually abstract, concepts in this category are frequently difficult to learn. Young children may show considerable confusion when told that the same town is north of one city and west of another.

Is this conjunctive, disjunctive, relational system of classification a particularly useful approach to understanding the nature and problems of concept formation? Closer examination suggests

9. R. M. W. Travers, *Essentials of Learning* (New York: Macmillan, 1963), p. 128.

that it is not. Disjunctive concepts on closer study turn out to be collections of conjunctive concepts. While an "out" in baseball, like a "down" in football seems to have the either/or characteristics that are supposed to distinguish disjunctive concepts, we frequently employ more precise terminology and speak of a player's having "grounded out," "flyed out," or been "forced out." Disjunctive concepts do not differ essentially from conjunctive concepts. There are two or more sets of characteristics in each disjunctive concept. They are, therefore, more complex than conjunctive concepts, and their greater difficulty may be accounted for on this basis alone.

Young children, it has often been noted, have difficulty with such questions as "How are an apple and a peach alike?" This difficulty has been attributed to the abstract nature of the concept "alike." However, the same child may have no trouble answering the question "How are an apple and a peach different?" Since both "alike" and "different" are relational concepts, the difficulty is obviously not inherent in the *type* of concept. If we examine the tasks confronting the child, we find that in answering the second question he is dealing with characteristics that are tangible and physically specifiable—that is, with fuzz versus a smooth skin, seeds versus a single pit, and the presence or absence of a stem. "Alike," at least in this instance, requires the child to deal with such intangibles as edibility, roundness, or the fact that both are fruit, in itself an abstraction.

A different approach to defining concept-formation tasks has been suggested by Goss.[10] He has pointed out that concept formation, fundamentally, requires *learning the same response to all members of a particular set of stimuli* and that these sets may be classified into three different types.

In the first type of concept-formation task, the stimuli exhibit variations in values along one or more physical or psychophysical dimensions, such as length, width, weight, or color. This type would be illustrated by the task in which a subject must learn to respond to the larger of two geometric shapes or by the more elaborate tests for brain damage in which subjects are required to categorize blocks that differ in size, shape, and color. (See Figure 4.)

10. A. E. Goss, "Verbal Mediating Responses and Concept Formation," *Psychological Review* (July 1961), pp. 248–74.

FIGURE 4

TYPE 1 CONCEPTS

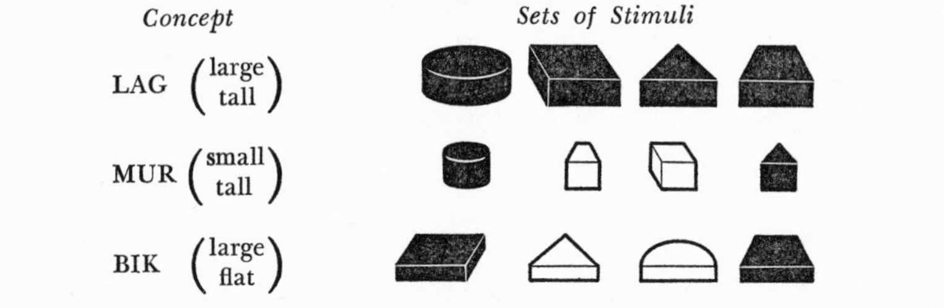

Concept	*Sets of Stimuli*
LAG (large tall)	
MUR (small tall)	
BIK (large flat)	

Distinguishing characteristics of the concept vary along one or more physical or psychophysical dimensions (size, color, etc.). Nonsense-syllable labels are used for the concepts to avoid giving subjects cues to the nature of the concept to be discovered.

SOURCE: Adapted from Eugenia Hanfmann and Jacob Kasanin, "A Method for the Study of Concept Formation," *Journal of Psychology,* Vol. III (1937).

Concepts of the second type consist of sets of stimuli in which there are one or more common elements, accompanied by other features that vary in an unsystematic fashion. (See Figure 5.) The common elements in this type of concept frequently cannot be defined along physical or psychophysical dimensions. We recognize, for example, that the concept "dog" refers to a category of ani-

FIGURE 5

TYPE 2 CONCEPTS

Concept	*Sets of Stimuli*
(ta)	
(hui)	
(na)	

All members of a conceptual category have (1) some specifiable element or relation in common and (2) other variable features. Neither common nor variable features can be completely reduced to physical or psychophysical dimensions.

SOURCE: Adapted from C. L. Hull, "Quantitative Aspects of the Evolution of Concepts," *Psychological Monographs,* Vol. XXVIII, No. 2 (1920), Whole No. 124.

mals, all of which have certain common characteristics. But we cannot specify these characteristics in inches, colors, or pounds.

The third type of concept is characterized by classes of stimuli that are not related to one another along common physical or psychophysical dimensions, that do not have any identifiable physical features in common, but that do elicit a common response. Figure 6 illustrates this type of concept.

Within each type of concept there are variations in difficulty, depending upon the number, complexity, and perceived differences among the stimuli. The concepts "pencil" and "amphibian" are both examples of our second type of concept, but "amphibian" is obviously the more difficult to acquire. In general, however, these three categories of concepts are increasingly abstract and in general are characterized by increased difficulty as we go from type 1 to type 3. Since language is critically important in acquiring type 3 concepts but of less importance in acquiring types 1 and 2, they also vary with respect to the increasing role played by verbal behavior in their acquisition.

FIGURE 6

TYPE 3 CONCEPTS

Concept	*Sets of Stimuli*			
round	barrel	doughnut	knob	balloon
white	bone	collar	frost	lint
sharp	needle	razor	splinter	knife

Sets of stimuli evoke a common response but cannot be reduced to common physical or psychophysical dimensions or defined by common elements or relations.

SOURCE: A. E. Goss, "Verbal Mediating Responses and Concept Formation," *Psychological Review* (July 1961).

Language and Concept Formation. Rats, chickens, apes, and other infrahuman organisms have been trained to respond consistently to such geometric forms as triangles, squares, or circles, even though the size or color of the form is changed from time to time. Such behavior would suggest that these animals, although incapable of verbal behavior, have grasped the abstract concepts of *squareness, triangularity,* or *circularity*. Osgood, however, has argued that a rat's ability to distinguish triangles of various sizes or colors from squares or circles does not constitute concept formation.[11] He contends that concept formation requires the learning of some common mediating response that is made to all sets of stimuli belonging to a particular conceptual category. Since it can be demonstrated that the rat will not respond positively to three dots versus four dots arranged in a square or to a three-cornered block versus a rectangular one, Osgood argues that the rat is not really responding to the abstract concept of triangularity, that he has not learned to make the same mediating response to all stimuli possessing this quality of triangularity.

Animals below the level of man appear capable also of making relational discriminations. If, for example, we train an animal to respond to the larger of two squares and then pair this square with a still larger square, he will respond to the larger of the two even though he has previously been reinforced for responding to what is now the smaller of the two squares. This *transposition behavior,* as it has been termed, has been considered by some psychologists as additional evidence that animals are able to learn such abstract concepts as "larger-than."

Spence, however, has offered another explanation for this behavior.[12] He has pointed out that when an organism responds to a particular stimulus and we reinforce him for doing so, his tendency to respond to that stimulus is increased. But there is also an increased likelihood that the organism will respond to *other* stimuli that are perceived as being similar to that one. This effect is known as *stimulus generalization.* The effects of extinction also generalize; when we extinguish a response to a particular stimulus we also reduce the organism's tendency to respond to other similar stimuli. Figure 7 illustrates how, according to Spence, the combined effects of stimulus generalization and generalization of extinction can result in an animal's appearing to make a relational discrimination.

In an experiment using chimpanzees as subjects, Spence paired stimulus squares 256 square centimeters in area with other squares 160 square centimeters in area. The chimpanzees were reinforced

11. C. E. Osgood, *Method and Theory in Experimental Psychology* (New York: Oxford University Press, 1953), pp. 667–68.
12. K. W. Spence, "The Differential Response in Animals to Stimuli Varying Within a Single Dimension," *Psychological Review* (September 1937), pp. 430–44.

FIGURE 7
TRANSPOSITION BEHAVIOR

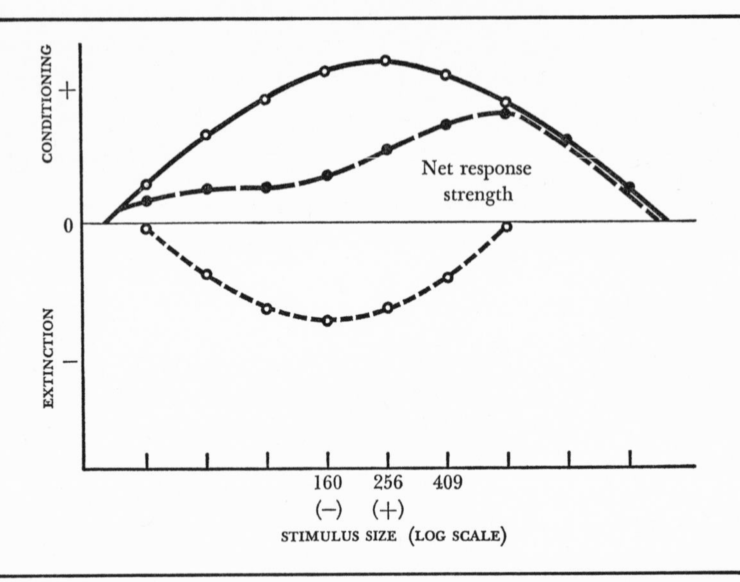

SOURCE: Adapted from K. W. Spence, "The Differential Response in Animals to Stimuli Varying Within a Single Dimension," *Psychological Review* (September 1937).

for responding to the larger squares. Responses to the smaller squares were extinguished. The upper curve in Figure 7 represents the effects of stimulus generalization and indicates that, as a result of reinforcing the 256-square-centimeter stimulus, the chimpanzees also acquired a strong tendency to respond to other stimuli of approximately the same size. This tendency declined as the stimulus was shifted farther away in either direction from stimuli of 256 square centimeters. Note, however, that the effect of extinguishing responses to the smaller square also generalized. Since the two stimulus squares are fairly near each other in size, extinguishing responses to the 160-centimeter stimulus also reduced the chimpanzees' tendency to respond to the 256-centimeter stimulus.

The net-response-strength curve indicates that the combined effects of reinforcement and extinction should result in a somewhat stronger tendency to respond to stimuli that are larger than 256 square centimeters. This is, in fact, what Spence found. After the chimpanzees had learned to choose the 256-square-centimeter stimulus in preference to one of 160 square centimeters, they were presented with squares having areas of 256 and 409 square centimeters; they chose the latter.

In support of Spence's explanation of transposition, other studies have shown that animals fail to show such behavior when the two initial stimuli are moved far apart. Under such circumstances, the effects of stimulus generalization and generalization of extinction overlap only slightly, if at all, and the animals continue to respond to the stimulus that was originally reinforced. Such evidence does not eliminate the possibility that animals that lack language are capable of genuine concept formation. However, it does make it unnecessary to assume that they are capable of acquiring abstract concepts such as triangularity or relative size.

Further support for Osgood's contention that the essential condition for concept formation is the learning of a common mediating response is seen in studies of children's behavior by Howard and Tracey Kendler.[13] Children in two age groups were presented with stimuli in the form of squares of two different sizes and colors. Their responses to the "correct" stimulus—to the larger square, for example, regardless of color—were reinforced. (See Figure 8.) After this response was established, two types of shift were made. In the *reversal shift,* if the child had been selecting the larger square, he now had to respond to the smaller square in order to be reinforced. Thus, size remained a relevant characteristic. In the *nonreversal* shift, size became irrelevant, and color, regardless of the size of the square, became the relevant cue.

When either a reversal or a nonreversal shift was made, the preschool children continued to respond to the previously correct stimulus for many trials. Their behavior resembled that of infrahuman subjects, in that a response, once established, had to be extinguished before a new response could be made. However, these younger children had less difficulty with nonreversal shifts, presumably because black and white stimuli had each been reinforced approximately the same number of times. The older children, when a reversal shift was made, shifted their response after a few trials. However, when a nonreversal shift was made, these older children had a great deal of difficulty discovering to which stimulus they should respond.

---

13. H. H. Kendler and T. S. Kendler, "Vertical and Horizontal Processes in Problem-Solving," *Psychological Review* (January 1962), pp. 1–16.

FIGURE 8

REVERSAL AND NONREVERSAL PROBLEMS

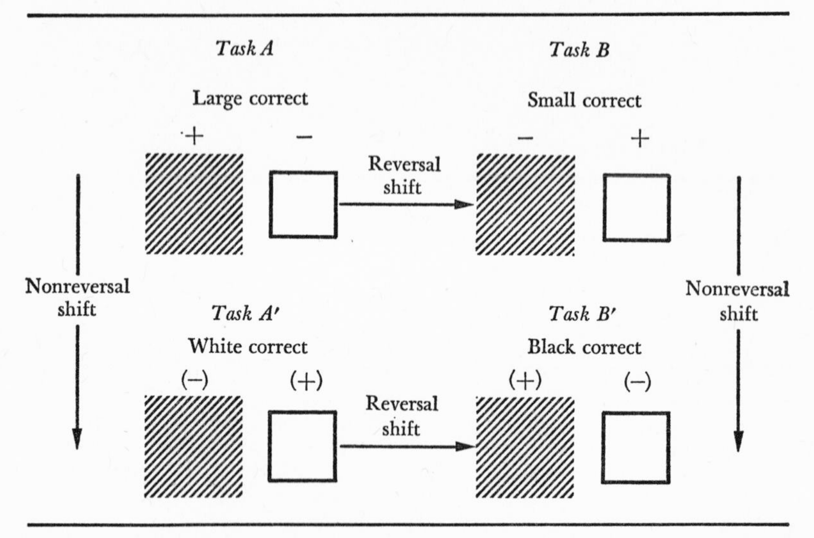

SOURCE: Adapted from H. H. Kendler and T. S. Kendler, "Vertical and Horizontal Processes in Problem-Solving," *Psychological Review* (January 1962).

It would appear that the younger children were responding directly to the stimuli, whereas the responses of the older children were mediated by some such intervening verbal response as "It's the larger one" or "Size is what counts." When a reversal shift was made, this mediating response still functioned to cue the older children to the relevant variable—size. But when the shift was from size to color, the mediated response handicapped them. The important point is that these older children were making their final response not directly to the stimulus but to an intermediate verbal response—the concept "size."

In our use of concepts, we frequently chain them together. Concepts linked together in a manner implying that there is a relatively stable relationship between them are referred to as *principles.* Such statements as "Bottles break" or "Water flows" are examples of relatively simple principles. The first could be made less restricted by substituting the concept "fragile objects" for "bottles," and the second could be made more precise by adding another concept, "downhill."

It does not seem necessary, however, to assume that learning principles differs fundamentally from learning concepts. Learning a principle requires learning two or more concepts, but this is also true of learning all but the simplest of concepts. Learning the concept "tree," for example, calls for first acquiring such concepts as "bark," "limbs," and "leaves." Moreover, it is possible to consider "breakability" as one of the attributes of bottles and fragile objects and "flowing" as a characteristic behavior of water. The same elements of discrimination and reinforcement that apply to learning concepts would seem to hold for the learning of principles.

Teaching and Concept Formation. At the basis of concept formation lies the ability to make appropriate discriminations among stimuli and to categorize these stimuli appropriately. For the parent and teacher, two questions arise: What can be done to improve discriminative ability? What kinds of experience facilitate categorization?

In seeking to answer these questions, psychologists have raised a more fundamental question: Is discrimination learning the result of a gradual improvement in performance over repeated trials, or does it really take the form of hypothesis testing? That is, does one's ability to discriminate improve slightly with each experience; or does the individual, in effect, say to himself, "It's probably that one," and have his choice confirmed or disproved? These two views have been designated, respectively, as the *continuity theory* and the *discontinuity theory*.

Experiments such as those conducted by the Kendlers suggest a third possibility. In the case of very young children or of infrahuman subjects, discrimination learning may be incremental. Each time a discriminative response is reinforced there is a gradual increase in the probability that the same discrimination will be made again. With older children, the ability to make covert verbal responses may result in a gradual shift to hypothesis testing. If further research should confirm this assumption, interesting questions will arise about the manner in which we attempt to teach concepts to children of varying levels of maturity.

Since concept formation requires the learner to categorize stimulus events, it necessitates multiple experiences. Repeating an identical experience cannot lead to concept formation. This fact is occasionally misunderstood or ignored by teachers who continue to repeat the same example or definition or who tell a confused student to "read it again." On the other hand, experiences can be so varied that the learner fails to identify the central elements. Acquisition of the concept "reptile" may be delayed rather than facilitated by presenting in the early stages of learning such disparate examples as a garter snake and a box turtle.

Concepts must be built carefully. The student learning the concept "feline" is handicapped unless he has already acquired the concepts of retractable claws and elliptical pupils, and the child who experiences difficulty in explaining how an apple and a peach are alike does so because he lacks such concepts as edibility, fruit, and roundness. Teachers who explain to third graders that the earth's interior is in a state of igneous fusion are probably bewildering the students rather than clarifying a concept.

Simplified examples are frequently used in teaching concepts. One frequent question has been the relative advantages of models and verbal descriptions as compared to "real life" experiences. For the teacher, there is no simple answer to this question. It is usually a matter of weighing one set of results against another. Taking a group of elementary-school students to visit a harbor may result in a "rich experience." On the other hand, it may result in their conceiving of a harbor as being compounded of hurrying people, loading cranes, noise, confusion, and strange odors—that is, in an abundance of connotative meaning and a shortage of denotative meaning.

Models, pictures, and verbal descriptions tend to emphasize critical elements by abstracting them for the learner and thereby simplifying his task. By modeling harbors on a sand table, showing children photographs of a number of different harbors, and pointing out the distinguishing characteristics of harbors, teachers may present the concept of harbor without the distractions offered by a real harbor. However, they may avoid the distraction of nonessential attributes at the price of oversimplifying the concept or of sacrificing some of the motivational effects of the actual experience. Simplifying experience tends to increase the speed with which concepts are acquired but may affect their accuracy. A combination of abstract and concrete experiences appears to be the most effective means of promoting concept formation, at least with older children and adults.

Educators have also pondered a related question: the relative merits of inductive versus deductive approaches to learning concepts and principles. Their discussions sometimes leave the impression that these approaches represent two different types of learning. In fact, deductive and inductive processes simply represent two different ways of arranging conditions to enable the learner to make the necessary discriminations among stimuli. In *deductive learning,* the identifying elements of the concept or principle to be learned are given to the learner, and opportunities are provided for him to recognize the concept or to apply the principle. Correct responses are then reinforced. In *inductive learning,* a variety of experiences are provided, all of which have some common conceptual element or employ a common principle. The learner's task is to identify the concept or discover the principle. These are sometimes referred to, respectively, as the *rule-given* approach and the *self-discovery* approach.

The relative effectiveness of inductive and deductive methods depends in part on the complexity of the concept, the capacity and experience of the learner, and the criteria one applies in judging the results. If we consider only the speed with which students can learn to define or identify a concept or principle and the clarity of their definitions, we find that the deductive method is generally superior. Some children, particularly the younger and the less able ones, frequently learn very slowly through an inductive approach, fail completely to grasp the concept, or are unable to define it with any precision. On the other hand, studies have indicated that motivation and retention are frequently higher when students learn inductively.

Whether experiences should include non-examples of the concept has also puzzled teachers. Non-examples—"This is an amphibian, *not* a reptile"—may sharpen and refine the learner's concepts and may serve as a test of his grasp of a concept. A salamander, for example, superficially resembles a lizard, and the child whose concept of "reptile" is inadequate may profit from having the critical differences pointed out to him. However, non-examples, particularly in the early stages of learning, may slow the process of concept formation, since they tend to convey less information than do positive instances of the concept. Consider the problem of learning what a book is by being shown only objects that are not books. Even where examples and non-examples have been equated experimentally for the amount of information conveyed by each, most individuals learn more rapidly from positive examples, perhaps as a result of an acquired preference for learning from examples rather than from non-examples.

In determining whether concepts have actually been learned, teachers often use tests calling for the student to give definitions of the concepts. Verbal behavior, as we have noted, plays an important role in concept formation, but the ability to memorize and repeat a group of words in a certain sequence is not identical with the ability to acquire a concept. Numerous studies have indicated that a student's ability to give a verbal definition is not a good indicator of an adequate understanding. Unfortunately, principles, too, can be learned simply as verbal chains. Many so-called principles, as learned by students, do not differ essentially from serial learning of nonsense syllables. Sometimes teachers present principles that, regardless of how they are learned, are inadequate or handicap the student at some later stage in his learning. Telling children that "Divide means make smaller" may be useful so long as they are dealing with whole numbers but will give rise to considerable confusion when fractions are encountered.

Concepts enable us in our thinking and learning to go beyond the stimulation of our immediate environment. Through our ability to acquire concepts we can manipulate objects, events, and experiences that are not immediately present; we can communicate with one another; and we can assimilate enormous amounts of knowledge. However, it is well to remind ourselves that, although language plays a very important role in concept formation, most concepts do have concrete references; they pertain to a real world. Many of our instructional procedures, however, are almost exclusively verbal, and it is possible for us to acquire concepts that are so attenuated, so removed from their referents, that they are useless or inadequate in helping us orient ourselves in our environment. For this reason, we should not overlook the importance of direct experience, of the laboratory and the demonstration, in the process of concept formation.

Suggestions for Class Discussion and Further Investigation

1. Mowrer has pointed out that young children *use* words before they *understand* them. What are some subtle examples of adults using words without really understanding them? How do you explain these occurrences?

2. Bugelski has commented that "Some teachers may be appalled by the prospect of students learning Italian, French, Spanish and Portuguese at the same time, yet, when there is a good reason for someone to learn these four languages, it well may be that he will do better learning them together than one at a time." Do you agree or disagree with this statement? Why?
3. If the anxieties of human beings can be aroused by verbal stimuli, do you think it is possible to extinguish these reactions by using other verbal stimuli, or must we go back to the experiences represented by the verbal symbols?
4. Is thinking the same thing as "talking to yourself"?
5. Comment on the following: A third grade pupil defined "cooperation" as "doing what the teacher tells you." How do you suppose he acquired this concept?
7. In using negative examples to help the learner refine his concepts, do you think it would be helpful if the negative examples were very similar to positive examples of the concept, or should they be quite different?
8. Several studies have found that people are able to use concepts they cannot define and that ability to define a concept is not necessarily indicative of ability to use the concept. What does this suggest to you about some of our evaluation procedures?

Suggestions for Further Reading

Language and Learning, 2nd ed. (1965), published by the *Harvard Educational Review,* contains nine articles covering the general topics of language learning, the learning of grammar and syntax, concept formation, and language disorders.

The Loom of Language, by Lancelot Hogben and F. Bodner (New York: Norton, 1944), provides an interesting, well-written background for those interested in the teaching and learning of language. Benjamin L. Whorf, *Language, Thought and Reality* (New York: Wiley, 1956), offers a different, but equally valuable, point of view.

In addition to presenting an S-R analysis of language development, Arthur and Carolyn Staats, *Complex Human Behavior* (New York: Holt, Rinehart and Winston, 1963), deals with the function of language in communication, reasoning and problem solving, mathematics, originality, and scientific behavior.

A condensed, but very readable, treatment of the psychology of language is presented in John B. Carroll, *Language and Thought* (Englewood Cliffs, N.J.: Prentice-Hall, Foundations of Modern Psychology Series, 1964).

The following two publications should be read by anyone interested in the problem of how children conceptualize their world: W. A. Brownell and G. Hendrickson, "How Children Learn Information, Concepts and Generalizations," in the Forty-Ninth Yearbook of the National Society for the Study of Education, Part I, *Learning and Instruction* (Chicago: University of Chicago Press, 1950), pp. 92–128; and Jean Piaget, *The Child's Conception of the World* (Paterson, N.J.: Littlefield Adams, 1960).

Roger Brown, *Words and Things* (Glencoe, Ill.: Free Press, 1958), and R. C. Johnson, "Linguistic Structure as Related to Concept Formation and to Concept Content," *Psychological Bulletin* (November 1962), pp. 468–76, consider the relationship of language and language forms to concept formation.

Chapter Six

Retention

"I forget."

This all-too-frequent response to a teacher's question often arouses other questions in the teacher's mind: Did the student really learn the material in the first place? If he did, why can't he remember it?

Each of us has had the experience of being unable to recall a name, an address, or the answer to a question, only to remember it later when we no longer needed it. What happens in these cases? What causes it to happen?

These are important questions for the teacher. As we noted in Chapter One, one of the fundamental concerns that teachers have about learning is whether or not their students will retain what they are learning for use outside the classroom and beyond the school years.

There are three possible explanations for breakdowns in retention. The first is a problem of storage; something occurs to change or eliminate responses that have been acquired. Second, there is a problem of retrieval; learned responses are not changed or extinguished, but we are unable to summon them up at the appropriate time, or we retrieve them in an incomplete or distorted fashion. Third, failures occur in both storage and retrieval processes.

Some of the response changes that occur in retention failures are *quantitative*. We can spell only half the words on a list, we can recall only the first three digits of a telephone number; or, in some cases, we fail to respond altogether. Other response changes are *qualitative* or *organizational*. Details of an experience may be dropped out and details from other experiences may be added, or material may be reorganized and remembered in a different form from that in which it was originally learned. Consider, for example, the following list of words:

tiger	carrot
potato	puma
spinach	leopard
wildcat	cabbage

If this list is memorized and retention is measured after some lapse of time, certain changes may be noted. Some of the words may not be recalled at all; there will probably also be a change in the order in which the words are recalled.

Retention is simplified if the words are grouped into two categories—*cats* and *vegetables*—and they will tend to be recalled that way. But these categorical headings may themselves arouse other responses, and we may find that "lion" or "mountain lion" is substituted for the less familiar "puma" when the list is recalled. The results of previous conditioning may also affect recall; those learners who associate "spinach" with unpleasant childhood experiences may recall more palatable vegetables.

PROBLEMS IN THE MEASUREMENT OF RETENTION

Experimental studies of retention are subject to certain limitations. Because of the difficulty of maintaining control over factors that might affect retention, most studies of retention have been conducted *over short periods of time.* Frequently, conditions are arranged to ensure that failures in retention will occur, since it would be impossible to study the comparative effects of the variables that affect retention if retention were perfect. The simplest way to do this is to prevent thorough learning of the material to be retained. Most of our experimental data on retention, therefore, is based on poorly learned material retained over short periods of time.

The methods used to measure retention also give rise to confusion in research on retention. Three principal procedures have been employed: recognition, recall, and relearning. *Recognition* requires that the subject demonstrate his retention by discriminating or identifying the material he has studied from other material. *Recall* requires that he reconstruct or reproduce what he has learned rather than simply identify it. *Relearning* calls for comparing the number of trials required for the initial learning of some response with the number of trials required, after a lapse of time, to relearn the same response. Sometimes comparisons are based on the number of errors made or the time required to learn and relearn rather than on the number of trials. If a subject requires fewer trials or makes fewer errors in relearning a response, it is reasonable to assume that he has retained something from the initial learning experience. While these first two methods are the basis for classroom examinations, *relearning* as a technique for measuring retention is rarely used outside experimental situations.

Each of these procedures tends to produce different results. Retention scores are usually highest when relearning and recognition are measured and lowest when recall is measured. Relearning sometimes indicates the persistence of memory when the other measures show no retention. Teachers who argue for one type of test over another should note that these differences do not reflect differences in retention itself; they simply indicate differences in the sensitivity of the measures.

THEORIES OF FORGETTING

What causes forgetting? When we try to answer this question, we find that it really becomes two questions: Is there some underlying process, something that happens to responses that we have acquired? What are the variables that affect retention?

Many people assume that forgetting is simply a matter of disuse—that responses, unless they are practiced, fade away like photographic proofs left too long in the sunlight. This view has been called the *trace theory,* on the assumption that memories are recorded in some form in the central nervous system and that forgetting results from the gradual eradication of memory traces from some unspecified location in the nervous system. Frequently used responses, it is suggested, would have more enduring traces. Though this view has some logical appeal, it does not stand up under investigation. Repetition *alone* does not guarantee retention. As we have noted, repeatedly evoking a response without reinforcement usually results in its being extinguished.

Psychologists have also attempted to explain some of the phenomena of forgetting on the basis of so-called *dynamic factors:*

the Freudian concept of repression, motivational differences, and the effect of attitudes toward particular subjects or events.

Most of us have had the experience of conveniently forgetting unpleasant events and tasks that we were not very eager to carry out. We can explain our forgetting in such instances as resulting from repression—that is, experiences that are threatening or disturbing are not permitted to come into consciousness. The forgotten material, according to this explanation, is not lost but has been rendered unavailable and cannot be recalled voluntarily.

Of course, we can also argue that such lapses of memory are not necessarily the result of unconscious processes but are due to a lack of motivation to remember or to negative attitudes toward the experiences. A number of studies have indicated that attitudes toward such topics as communism or minority groups markedly affect what is retained from material presented on these subjects.

Underlying all these explanations may be a common factor: poor initial learning. Material that is unpleasant, threatening, and anxiety provoking will probably be learned less well than pleasant or neutral material. A lack of interest in learning certain material may also result in poor initial learning and, consequently, in poor retention. The effects of attitudes on retention may be explained on the same basis: material that is radically different from, or that conflicts with, previous learning cannot be so readily attached to well-established associations. This suggests that our motives—conscious or unconscious—and our attitudes affect what we learn and, therefore, what we retain from our experiences.

A more widely accepted and more general explanation of forgetting is the *interference,* or *competition,* theory. According to this view, failures of retention result from the interference, or competition, of other responses with the desired response. This competition may manifest itself in several ways: the recall of an incorrect response, increased reaction time before the correct response is made, the depression of all alternative responses and the arousal of some irrelevant response, or a complete failure to respond.

One source of interference is *retroactive inhibition,* which occurs when an interpolated learning activity affects the retention of some previously learned response. J. G. Jenkins and K. M. Dallenbach, in a study carried out in 1924,[1] arranged for two students

---

1. J. G. Jenkins and K. M. Dallenbach, "Obliviscence During Sleep and Waking," *American Journal of Psychology* (October 1924), pp. 605–12.

to learn lists of nonsense syllables. The first night, one student immediately went to sleep and was awakened and tested after an hour's sleep. On each of three succeeding nights he learned a new list and was awakened and tested—on the second night after two hours, on the third after four hours, and on the fourth after eight hours. The second subject continued his usual waking activities after he had memorized the lists and was tested after the same intervals as the first student. At each testing point, the sleeping subject had higher retention scores, and his scores varied little after different intervals of sleep. The scores of the subject who remained awake declined as the intervals between learning and testing increased. The differences in retention between these subjects appeared to be due to the fact that the student who remained awake had more opportunity to learn competing or interfering responses between the initial task and the test of retention.

The effect of a previously learned response upon the learning and retention of a new response is termed *proactive inhibition.* Two basic designs for measuring the effects of proactive and retroactive inhibition follow:

Proactive inhibition
 Experimental group
  Learns task A . . . Learns task B . . . Tested on task B
 Control group
  Rests . . . . . . Learns task B . . . Tested on task B

Retroactive inhibition
 Experimental group
  Learns task A . . . Learns task B . . . Tested on task A
 Control group
  Learns task A . . . Rests . . . . . . Tested on task A

In experiments with human subjects, there is always the possibility, particularly with a retroactive design, that the control group may practice task A during the rest period. To prevent this, the members of the control group are often kept busy during this period on some unrelated task.

The potentially disruptive effects of interpolated learning—that is, of retroactive interference—are quite obvious and understandable to most people. As it turns out, however, proactive interference probably plays a more important role in human forgetting. Underwood noticed that studies of retention in different laboratories reported varying percentages of material recalled, although the types of material used and the experimental procedures employed were essentially the same. He discovered, however, that the subjects employed in the experiments differed in the amount of previous experience they had had in memorizing lists. There was a clear relationship between percentage of material retained and amount of experience. Those subjects who had previously memorized the greatest number of lists showed the lowest rates of retention when they memorized new lists. Apparently, the previously learned lists interfered with the recall of the more recently learned lists.[2]

Since we are constantly learning new responses, why does retention not break down entirely as a result of the competition and interference of learned responses with one another? As a matter of fact, our memories do suffer. Parents are frequently startled when one of their children says "Remember when . . . ?" and proceeds to describe some past event in minute detail, an event the parents remember vaguely, if at all. Such amazing retention is probably due to the fact that the child has a shorter span of experience and, as a consequence, suffers less from proactive interference.

There are two major reasons why retention is not completely overwhelmed by the cumulative effect of competing responses. First, we are constantly practicing the more important responses. Second, we acquire techniques for keeping important responses from competing with one another.

To attribute failures of retention to the interference of one learned response with another is, of course, to provide only the scantiest of explanations, one that leaves many important questions unanswered. Once we have moved beyond infancy, every response we learn is, at least theoretically, subject to the effects of proactive inhibition. Yet we continue to learn and retain, and many of our responses are not forgotten even though they go unpracticed for months or years. Why is it that some of the things we learn seem to be retained indefinitely, while others are quickly forgotten? Does the difference lie in the nature of the material learned, in the manner in which it is learned, or in the relationship of one learned response to another?

---

2. B. J. Underwood, "Interference and Forgetting," *Psychological Review* (January 1957), pp. 49–60.

VARIABLES RELATED TO RETENTION

Nature of the Material. Since we do tend to forget some things very rapidly, while retaining other responses over long periods of time, several psychologists have tried to determine whether some types of learning are less subject to interference than others.

Jenkins and Dallenbach, in their study of retention during sleep and waking, used nonsense syllables and found significantly greater retention when their subjects went to sleep immediately following learning.[3] Newman, however, found that the effects of a period of sleep or activity following learning depended upon the type of material that had been learned.[4] Subjects were given stories containing "essential" and "nonessential" material to memorize. After eight hours of sleep the essential material was retained with 87 percent accuracy and the nonessential material with 47 percent accuracy. What is more significant is that other subjects, who remained awake and active during this eight-hour period, showed no greater loss of retention of the essential material than did those who had slept; their retention of nonessential material, however, dropped to 25 percent.

Newman's study does not refute the idea that forgetting results from the interference of other activities and experiences, but it does suggest that some types of material are more resistant than others to interference. This viewpoint is supported by another study [5] in which it was found that observational material and poetry were both retained significantly better than nonsense material.

Reorganization and Recoding. Finding that some learned responses are more readily retained than others has some practical value. It enables us to anticipate some of the difficulties that students may encounter in trying to retain certain types of materials. But it would be even more helpful if we were able to understand why these differences exist.

One explanation that has been offered is that some materials are more readily *reorganized* or *recoded* than others. In consider-

---

3. *Loc. cit.*
4. E. B. Newman, "Forgetting of Meaningful Material During Sleep and Waking," *American Journal of Psychology* (January 1939), pp. 65–71.
5. A. R. Gilliland, "The Rate of Forgetting," *Journal of Educational Psychology,* Vol. XXXIX (1948), pp. 19–26.

ing our list of vegetables and wild members of the cat family, we noted that changes, in the form of reorganization of this material, would probably take place if we attempted to recall it after a period of time. We would tend to simplify it and bring it closer into line with our previous experiences. We should also note that reorganization is not only something that happens *to* retained material, it is also *a factor affecting retention.*

George A. Miller, in an intriguing article, "The Magical Number Seven, Plus or Minus Two," [6] has pointed out that there are definite limits to our ability to receive, process, and remember information. He notes that most of us can deal with about seven categories in making judgments, that our attention span will take in approximately seven items, and that our span of immediate memory will allow us to retain about the same number of digits or isolated letters. However, Miller distinguishes between what he refers to as *bits* of information and *chunks* of information. Although our immediate recall for isolated letters is limited, we can organize letters into words, or chunks. And we can organize words into still larger chunks, into ideas or sentences. This process, in the language of communication theory, is called *recoding.* Essentially, we are recoding the input into another form that contains more bits per chunk and fewer chunks.

Miller believes that, while we are limited to a relatively constant number of chunks, the span of immediate memory is almost independent of the number of bits per chunk. As the data in Figure 9 indicate, where the number of items (chunks) is held constant, the amount of information retained by the learner increases as a linear function of the number of bits of information contained in each item. For example, individuals asked to retain seven or eight items, each item containing five digits or letters, remembered approximately twice as many digits as did those who were required to memorize the same number of two-digit or two-letter items. This suggests that we can increase retention by loading more separate bits of information into each chunk, provided we do not ask the learner to memorize more chunks of information than his span of retention can encompass.

Theories such as Miller's suggest a number of intriguing possibilities. Ever since Ebbinghaus's experiments, we have been aware

---

6. *Psychological Review* (March 1956), pp. 81–97.

FIGURE 9

AMOUNT OF INFORMATION RETAINED
AS A FUNCTION OF THE NUMBER OF BITS
OF INFORMATION PRESENTED IN EACH ITEM

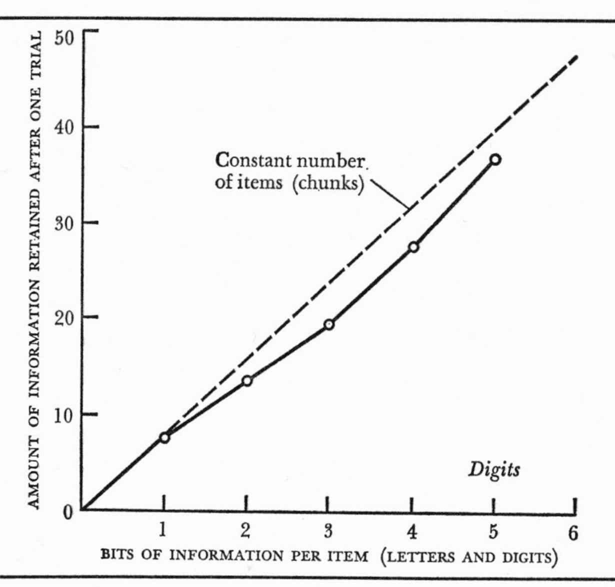

SOURCE: Data from I. Pollack, "The Assimilation of Sequentially Encoded Information," *American Journal of Psychology,* Vol. 66 (1953).

that nonsense syllables are not retained well and that such isolated facts as names, dates, or technical terminology are forgotten almost as rapidly. On the other hand, "meaningful" material—descriptive statements, stories, and concepts—frequently are well retained over extended periods of time. One explanation is that meaningful material is more highly organized. Unlike lists of nonsense syllables or isolated facts and terms, many separate bits of information have been recoded into a relatively small number of chunks. The reactions of many people to the digit-dialing systems adopted by telephone companies may be explained on the same basis. The number JAckson 3–9016 presents us with six bits to be retained, a word and five digits. However, when this is converted to 523–9016 it approaches the limit of the retention span of many people. Adding a three-digit area code may seriously overtax their retentive capacities and force them to group these separate digits into several chunks of three or four digits each. Without being fully aware of the basis for their distress, people protesting against the anonymity of digit dialing may really be reacting to the stress such a system places upon their capacities for retention.

Recoding may also take the form of *labeling*—attaching some familiar name to an object or an event that, because of its unfamiliarity or complexity, may be difficult to recall. Carmichael, Hogan, and Walter, in an early study,[7] presented subjects with a series of stimulus forms, which they were later asked to recall. Figure 10 indicates the effects upon recall of attaching different labels to the same form. Such studies suggest that coding in the form of labeling may improve retention, particularly when it gives meaning to ambiguous stimuli. It is also apparent, however, that this type of coding can result in distortion, suggesting that labels must be accurate if they are to function as aids to memory.

It would appear that our capacities for retention are rather definitely limited. If this is the case, the most profitable approach to improved retention may be to improve systems of recoding rather than to attempt to increase the learner's retention span. For the teacher, this approach offers two possibilities: (1) organizing and presenting material so that it is easily recoded by the learner into few enough units to fall within his retention span and (2) helping learners perceive and develop useful techniques for recoding the material that they must learn and retain.

One obvious way to reorganize material is to convert isolated facts into principles or generalizations wherever this is possible. Katona compared subjects who were taught a principle for memorizing a series of numbers with another group who learned the same series on a rote basis.[8] Not only did the first group learn more efficiently, but their retention at the end of three weeks was significantly better. Tyler found that students in a college biology course showed sharp drops in the amount of factual material retained when tested a year after the completion of the course.[9]

7. L. Carmichael, H. P. Hogan, and A. A. Walter, "An Experimental Study of the Effect of Language on the Reproduction of Visually Perceived Form," *Journal of Experimental Psychology*, Vol. XV (1932), pp. 73–86.

8. G. Katona, *Organizing and Memorizing* (New York: Columbia University Press, 1940).

9. R. Tyler, "Some Findings from Studies in the Field of College Biology," *Science Education*, XVIII (1934), 133–42.

FIGURE 10

EFFECT OF VERBAL LABELS UPON RECALL

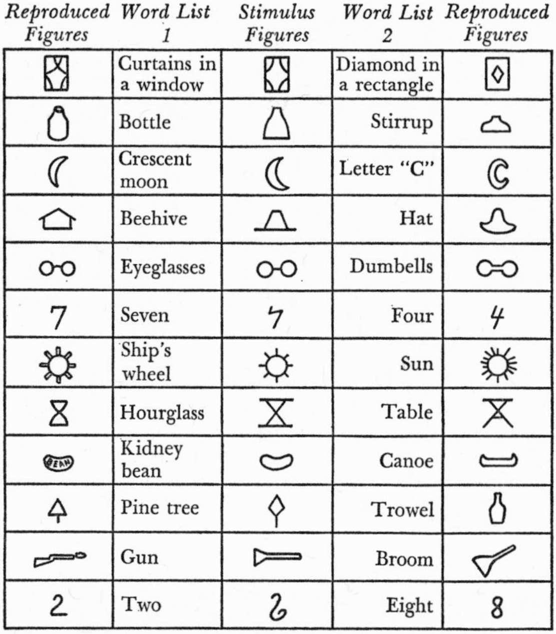

Reproduced Figures	*Word List 1*	*Stimulus Figures*	*Word List 2*	*Reproduced Figures*
	Curtains in a window		Diamond in a rectangle	
	Bottle		Stirrup	
	Crescent moon		Letter "C"	
	Beehive		Hat	
	Eyeglasses		Dumbells	
7	Seven	7	Four	4
	Ship's wheel		Sun	
	Hourglass		Table	
	Kidney bean		Canoe	
	Pine tree		Trowel	
	Gun		Broom	
2	Two	2	Eight	8

Subjects tended to reproduce drawings resembling the words they had associated with the stimulus figures.

SOURCE: Adapted from L. Carmichael, H. P. Hogan, and A. A. Walter, "An Experimental Study of the Effect of Language on the Reproduction of Visually Perceived Form," *Journal of Experimental Psychology,* Vol. XV (1932).

On the other hand, these students were somewhat better able to apply the principles they had learned to new experiments a year later than they had been immediately following the completion of the course. These results may be due in part to the fact that the pieces of information in a principle are highly organized—that is, interrelated with one another. Recalling one part of the principle may result in recall of the remainder.

Studies such as Tyler's suggest that teachers may unwittingly influence retention through the tests they use to evaluate student achievement. If facts are stressed in tests, this is what students, in self-defense, will learn. They will have less tendency to learn principles or generalizations, and overall retention may be seriously impaired. This is not meant to suggest that facts or technical terminology are always unimportant. Often they are extremely important, and, since they are frequently difficult to learn and to retain, special attention should be given to problems of learning and retaining them. However, there is little danger in most schools that the learning of names, dates, definitions, and formulae will be slighted. Teachers find it much easier to write questions based on such material than to test students' ability to understand and apply principles. Consequently, students have little incentive to organize or to seek meaningful relationships among the isolated pieces of information they learn.

The Total Stimulus Pattern. As we have noted, human beings frequently show an amazing ability to focus on certain stimuli and to adapt out or ignore other stimuli that seem irrelevant. Nevertheless, we apparently do respond to overall patterns of stimulation, probably more frequently than we respond to a single, isolated stimulus.

The fact that we respond to patterns of stimulation may account for differences between the results of laboratory research on retention and what seems to happen outside the laboratory. It also sheds some light on a number of other occurrences: the child who recites his Mother's Day "piece" letter-perfect in the family living room or the classroom but becomes tongue-tied in the auditorium; well-prepared students who fail to answer questions when queried by a classroom visitor; the adolescent who forgets to use his napkin when dining in a restaurant or at a party. In each case, the individual has learned under one pattern of stimulation, but the stimulus pattern under which he is called upon to perform has been changed sufficiently so that the response is not elicited.

A similar but less obvious situation occurs when teachers frame examination questions in unfamiliar terms. Their intentions may be good; they wish to avoid "sheer memorization" and to promote "understanding." However, these are expressions that teachers should scrutinize carefully and unemotionally. What we know of stimulus generalization leads us to expect that the learner will respond in the same manner to stimuli that he perceives as being similar and that this tendency will decline as the stimuli become increasingly dissimilar. There is little reason to expect that a student who has learned to respond to one pattern of stimulation will automatically make the same response to a changed pattern simply because the *teacher* perceives them as being related.

The implications are fairly obvious: we must either teach the learner under conditions that are highly similar to those under which we later expect him to perform, or, since this is frequently impossible, we must arrange for him to learn under varied conditions of stimulation. We should not expect that, having learned to respond appropriately to one stimulus pattern, he will, in some mysterious fashion, come to "understand" that this response may also be appropriately made to other patterns of stimulation.

Degree of Learning. The results of both laboratory research and our everyday observations agree on one point: well-learned responses are less subject to interference and, therefore, are retained better than poorly or partially learned responses. Army serial numbers, a frequently called telephone number, the letters of the alphabet—all are likely to be retained perfectly for many years.

One reason is that responses of this sort have been *overlearned*—that is, they have been repeatedly practiced *after* the point of simple mastery has been reached. Overlearning is particularly important in learning and retaining material that is acquired on the basis of simple associations such as "red means stop," or "*b* follows *a*." Unfortunately, most students are reluctant to continue practicing once they have achieved what they consider to be mastery of the material. In most instances, "mastery" means to the student going through a spelling list or a representative problem once with no errors.

Figure 11 indicates that students who overlearned lists of nouns by 50 percent showed significantly higher levels of retention than did students who stopped practice as soon as they attained mastery.[10] One-hundred percent overlearning—that is, spending as much time after learning as before—resulted in a still higher level of retention. We noted that highly organized materials, such as principles, tend to be retained better than isolated facts. An additional reason for their greater retention may be that principles, having more generality than facts, are applicable in a greater number of situa-

10. W. C. F. Kreuger, "The Effect of Overlearning on Retention," *Journal of Experimental Psychology* (February 1929), pp. 71–78.

FIGURE 11

EFFECTS OF OVERLEARNING ON RETENTION

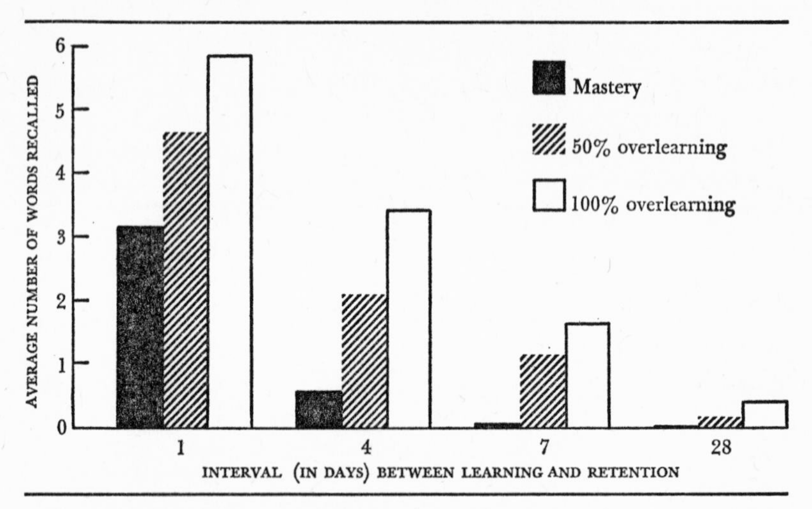

SOURCE: Data from W. C. F. Kreuger, "The Effect of Overlearning on Retention," *Journal of Experimental Psychology* (February 1929).

tions. Therefore, they are likely to be more frequently applied (practiced), with the result that they become overlearned.

A common bit of educational folklore is that the student who learns slowly and painfully in some way learns more thoroughly and has better retention than the student who learns quickly and easily. A number of psychologists have pointed out that, contrary to this belief, there is a *positive* relationship between speed of learning and retention. However, the situation is somewhat more complex than this last statement would indicate. If we analyze what occurs during practice, we note that not only can the faster learner cover a given amount of material more quickly and, if we do not limit the number of trials, cover it more times, but he probably also makes more correct responses. As Underwood has pointed out, a correct response apparently strengthens an association more for a fast learner than for a slow one.[11] Fast learners, then, do not have an inherently greater ability to remember things,

11. B. J. Underwood, "Speed of Learning and Amount Retained: A Consideration of Methodology," *Psychological Bulletin* (May 1954), pp. 276–82.

but they profit more from practice and do learn more thoroughly. This thoroughness of learning probably accounts for their superior retention.

Intent. Practice appears to be a significant element in retention. But practice in the form of mere exposure to the material to be learned is not sufficient to ensure high levels of retention. Retention appears to be markedly affected by the learner's *intent,* both to learn and to retain. The two-pack-a-day smoker, for example, can usually give only a very inadequate description of the tax stamp on a package of cigarettes, although he has seen it hundreds of times. But he has, of course, no real interest in acquiring or retaining this particular information. Probably a major reason we do not retain material better than we do is because we do not really intend either to learn the material thoroughly or to retain it. We usually plan to reread or restudy it more carefully and thoroughly if the necessity should arise. Students taking notes during a lecture, for example, are usually not set to retain what is being said; they plan to return to their notes later on. But notes, unless they are very comprehensive, do not fully cover the material presented; they merely serve as cues to stimulate our recall. If too much time elapses between note-taking and recall, or if we fail to attend to the rest of the lecture while taking notes on certain points, gaps in retention will result. One solution would be to take less detailed notes but to review them shortly after they have been taken, while they can still serve as stimuli for recall of a major portion of the material.

The general picture of retention may appear depressing. Our memories are far from perfect under the best of conditions, and conditions are rarely optimal. We can improve retention through overlearning, by developing more effective systems of recoding and reorganizing, and by *intending* to retain what we are learning. Teachers can also influence retention through the types of student evaluation they use. But we must still expect considerable losses, particularly over extended periods of time. There is, however, one redeeming factor: *the efficiency of relearning.* Once we have learned something, even though we may be unable to retrieve a great deal of it at some later date, we can usually relearn it then with far fewer trials than were required for the initial learning.

It may be true that the more we learn, the more we forget. But it is also true that the more we learn, the greater our ability to relearn quickly and efficiently.

Suggestions for Class Discussion and Further Investigation

1. What are some ways in which you might apply overlearning to some of your present studies? In the case of some courses, could you be sure that you were really overlearning and not learning something additional?
2. Can we really separate relearning from recall? If a student relearns material more rapidly or with fewer trials, how can we be sure this is not due to his having recalled more?
3. Are there any principles that could be taught to students to assist them in recoding or reorganizing a wide variety of material for better retention?
4. It has been suggested that students might learn more if they studied one subject at a time, devoting all their time to that subject before taking up another one. What effect do you think this procedure would have upon retention?
5. Attempt to summarize what you have retained from the first two chapters of this book. Are there any differences between the two chapters in the amount you have retained? How do you account for this?
6. Do you think some types of material are intrinsically more difficult to retain than others? Or is it that these materials are more difficult to *learn?*

Suggestions for Further Reading

Most studies of retention have concentrated on the effects of one or a very few variables on retention. However, Benton J. Underwood, "Forgetting," *Scientific American* (March 1964), pp. 91–99, is an excellent general discussion of this topic.

M. D. Sterrett and R. A. Davis provide a relatively brief review of research up to 1954 on the retention of classroom learning in their article "The Permanence of School Learning: A Review of Studies," *Educational Administration and Supervision* (December 1954), pp. 449–60.

Although less specifically related to the classroom, other helpful articles are Leslie J. Briggs and Nancy R. Hamilton, "Meaningful Learning and Retention: Practice and Feedback Variables," *Review of Educational Research* (December 1964), pp. 545–58, and J. H. Reynolds and R. Glaser, "Effects of Repetition and Spaced Review upon Retention of a Complex Learning Task," *Journal of Educational Psychology* (October 1964), pp. 297–308.

Several books have been written containing suggestions for the improvement of retention. Two of the better ones are: C. T. Morgan and J. E. Deese, *How to Study* (New York: McGraw-Hill, 1957); and F. P. Robinson, *Effective Study* (New York: Harper & Row, 1946).

Chapter Seven

Transfer

Is the study of Latin helpful in learning French? Should children be taught phonics as a first step in teaching them to read? Do habits of neatness in doing arithmetic assignments carry over to keeping a checkbook in order? Is a liberal education a better preparation for the future than technical training?

Such questions have bedeviled teachers and others concerned with education for years and have provoked some of our sharpest educational disputes. Recently, for example, there has been a great deal of debate, much of it acrimonious, over the effect of teacher-education programs on the subsequent performance of teachers in the classroom. The question of whether phonics should be taught as a first step in learning to read has been argued in several books and in scores of articles.

All these questions reduce, fundamentally, to one: Does some instance of learning have an influence, positive or negative, upon subsequent learning, relearning, or performance? In short, they are all questions about *transfer of learning.*

It is quite apparent that learning does transfer, which is most fortunate, since transfer not only is important in increasing the efficiency of learning but is essential to the development and survival of higher forms of life, including man. If learning did not transfer, we could not profit from previous experiences. Each time we encountered a new situation we would have to learn again from the beginning. Consequently, adaptation to anything but an unchanging environment would be virtually impossible. Our entire system of education, both formal and informal, would be completely pointless, because it is predicated on the fact that learning does transfer, that learning that occurs in one situation—

in the classroom, for example—will facilitate performance or learning under other conditions.

While the fact of transfer is inescapable, there remain many questions *about* transfer: How much transfer actually occurs? Do some types of learning transfer more readily than others? What are the variables that affect transfer? What can be done to increase transfer? Does transfer always facilitate subsequent learning or performance, or is there such a thing as negative transfer?

Much of our difficulty in studying these problems of transfer stems from the fact that virtually every learning situation is a transfer situation. By the time a child reaches school age, it is almost impossible to find a learning task that is not, to some extent, affected by previous experiences.

Viewed in this light, readiness is basically a matter of transfer, a question of whether there is sufficient transfer from a child's previous experiences to permit him to cope with present learning tasks. If he cannot make the necessary transfer from the previous learning to the new, we can either modify his experiential background or change the nature of the task. Many of the attempts to increase the educability of children from urban and rural slum areas have adopted the first approach. Other efforts, such as the Initial Teaching Alphabet, the experiments of O. K. Moore in teaching preschool children to type and read simultaneously, and some of the programs in science, mathematics, and foreign-language instruction for elementary-school children, have tried to modify the task so that the children's present backgrounds will be adequate. These experimental programs suggest that we should consider readiness in terms of readiness for a particular mode of instruction. They also suggest that simply waiting for the learner to "mature" is hardly the answer to problems of readiness, unless we can be sure that the necessary experiences will inevitably occur with the passage of time.

In a somewhat less direct fashion, some motivational problems, too, are probably related to transfer. Hunt maintains that a basic reason for the lack of interest in learning displayed by some children is that we do not match their experiences very well with the learning tasks we give them.[1] When we present learners with im-

1. J. McV. Hunt, "Implications of Piaget's Stages for Matching Circumstances and Schemata," *Intelligence and Experience* (New York: Ronald, 1961), pp. 273–88.

possible or excessively difficult transfer tasks we may frustrate, bewilder, or bore them.

Any discussion of transfer, therefore, inevitably involves us—or entangles us—in a consideration of other aspects of learning, such as retention, the effects of experience and practice upon learning, motivation, or verbal mediation. Conversely, when we consider such topics as concept formation, problem solving, or learning sets, we find that each of these is a special instance of transfer.

Since transfer is concerned with the effects of some previous experience on subsequent learning or behavior, there is an obvious relationship between transfer and retention. We can transfer only what we retain. Consequently, we would expect that those variables that have an effect on retention would also have an effect on transfer. There are, however, some differences between retention and transfer.

Typically, in the case of retention, we are interested in whether the learner, having acquired some response is able to make this same response, appropriately, at some later time. With transfer of learning, we are less concerned with whether he can make this same response again than with the *effect* upon subsequent learning of his having learned it. The student who can recite a poem several years after learning it or who can quote long passages of prose is demonstrating retention. However, most teachers of literature contend that they are less interested in the retention of a particular poem or drama than in the effects that studying these works have upon the student's later appreciation and judgment of literature.

THEORIES OF TRANSFER

Educators have long observed that students who did well in the more difficult academic subjects were particularly adept at solving problems, tended to be logical and orderly in their thought processes, and were in general superior learners. From these observations the *mental-discipline* theory of transfer evolved. The mind, according to this theory, is analogous to a muscle; vigorous exercise strengthens it. Pupils were encouraged to study mathematics and Latin, not because they were expected to have a great many future occasions to use their ability to read Cicero or solve quadratic equations, but because these studies were more "rigorous" than home economics or geography and resulted in more strenuous mental exercise.

Unfortunately, those who claimed to find support for this view of transfer sometimes overlooked the fact that many of the students who studied Latin, geometry, and algebra were initially more able than those who went into home-economics or business-arithmetic classes. Some of Thorndike's early research indicated that transfer was no greater for "rigorous" subjects than for subjects supposedly less intellectually demanding. According to Thorndike, transfer depended not on strengthening the mind but on the existence of *identical elements* in both the original task and the transfer task. Those who subscribed to Thorndike's theory generally interpreted this to mean that, unless there were identical *stimulus elements* in the two situations and unless these were perceived by the learner, transfer would not occur. They largely overlooked the possibility that the identical elements in two situations could include identical attitudes or study habits or the similar use of materials and techniques.

Most current theorizing about the nature and conditions of transfer has descended directly from the identical-elements position. However, research—particularly research on learning sets or "learning to learn"—suggests that factors other than identical-stimulus elements may affect transfer. The learner may acquire some general principle and respond to this principle rather than to the specific stimuli in a situation.

Psychologists have developed a number of models to describe the stimulus-response relationships that affect transfer. One of the better known of these models was developed by C. E. Osgood (Figure 12). Any degree of response similarity and stimulus similarity between two tasks can be represented by a single point on the rectangular plane. The amount of transfer expected from a particular combination of response and stimulus similarity can be estimated by extending a perpendicular from the point on the plane to the curved surface. If the point on the curved surface is above the plane, positive transfer is predicted; if it is below the plane, negative transfer is predicted.

Osgood's transfer surface indicates that the greatest amount of positive transfer should occur when stimuli and responses are identical or very similar in both the old learning situation and the new, or transfer, situation. Thus we might expect the student

FIGURE 12
OSGOOD'S TRANSFER SURFACE

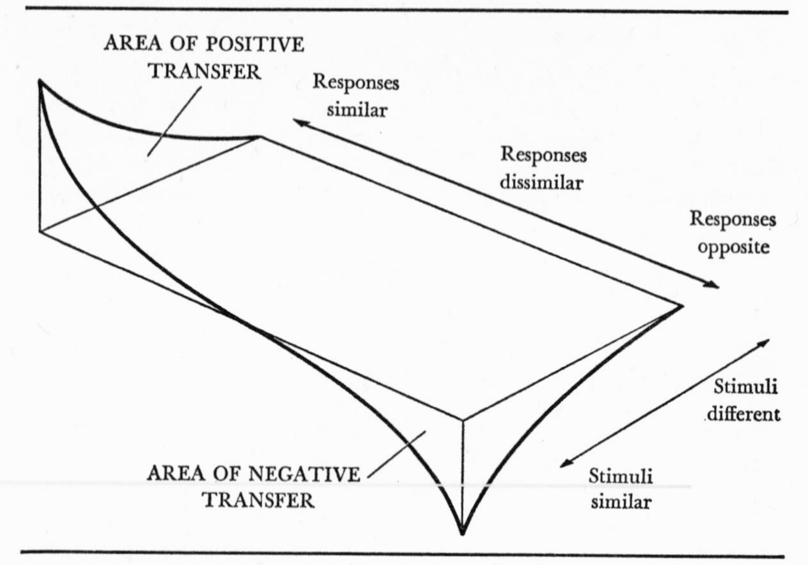

The amount of transfer (positive and negative) is a joint function of the relationship between response similarity and stimulus similarity of the original task and the transfer task. Adapted from C. E. Osgood, "The Similarity Paradox in Human Learning: A Resolution," *Psychological Review* (May 1949), pp. 132–43.

who has previously learned in Latin class that *"aquila"* means "eagle" to show some positive transfer when he meets the word "aquiline" in an English-vocabulary list. Negative transfer should occur when the stimuli in the new situation are similar to those in the original learning situation but call for a different response. If, for example, a student who has learned that "inane" means "silly" perceives "inane" and "innate" as being equivalent stimuli, we can anticipate negative transfer. Where both stimuli and responses in learning and transfer situations are completely different, Osgood's model would predict no transfer effect, a not very surprising outcome. We would not expect that practicing the piano or conjugating irregular French verbs would have much effect upon learning to swim.

Although Osgood's transfer surface seems to fit these and many other examples of transfer, we should apply these stimulus-response relationships with considerable caution. Osgood's model is adequate for the data available at the time it was formulated (1949), but a number of more recent studies have reported results that do not fit or that actually contradict these predictions. This suggests that in some transfer situations these stimulus-response relationships either do not prevail or are overwhelmed by the effects of other variables in the situation. Bugelski and Cadwallader found that a greater amount of negative transfer occurred when subjects were required to learn similar but not identical responses than when the new responses were neutral or opposing.[2] Deese and Hardman presented subjects with stimuli consisting of incomplete sentences, such as "The path is . . . ." [3] As responses, they had to learn words that completed these sentences—for example, the word "rocky." After learning the appropriate response to each incomplete sentence, the subjects were required to learn a new set of responses. Half the subjects, however, had to learn new responses that were synonymous with the old responses; "stony," for example, might become the new completion for "The path is . . . ." The other half of the subjects learned a new list of words unrelated to the original completions; "short," for example, might replace "rocky." The results up to this point agreed with the predictions that might be made from Osgood's transfer surface. There was positive transfer from the original list of completions to the synonyms and negative transfer to the unrelated words. However, when the experimenters required all the subjects to relearn the original list of completions, those who had learned the list of synonyms had considerably greater difficulty relearning the original responses. This result would not be predicted by Osgood's model.

Deese and Hardman believe that the synonyms, being easier to learn than the unrelated words, were learned more thoroughly. Therefore, they competed more with the original responses, and those subjects who learned the synonyms did not retain the original responses as well as did those subjects who learned unrelated (and

2. B. R. Bugelski and T. C. Cadwallader, "A Reappraisal of the Transfer and Retroaction Surface," *Journal of Experimental Psychology* (December 1956), pp. 360–66.
3. J. Deese and G. W. Hardman, Jr., "An Analysis of Errors in Retroactive Inhibition of Rote Verbal Learning," *American Journal of Psychology,* Vol. LXVII (1954), pp. 299–307.

noncompeting) words. These results, when explained in this way, are not incompatible with the transfer surface, but obviously one should be cautious about uncritical generalizations from this model. Both this experiment and the one by Bugelski and Cadwallader followed a retroactive design. (See Figure 13.) It would appear

FIGURE 13

DESIGNS FOR PROACTIVE AND RETROACTIVE TRANSFER EXPERIMENTS

Proactive Transfer Design		
Experimental groups		
Group 1: Learns Latin		Learns French
Group 2: Learns German		Learns French
Group 3: Learns Spanish		Learns French
Control group		
Group 4: Rests		Learns French
Retroactive Transfer Design		
Experimental group		
Learns to water ski	Skis on snow	Water skis
Control group		
Learns to water ski	Rests	Water skis

In both designs, experimental and control groups are compared on the basis of performance on the final (transfer) task.

to be less hazardous to apply the transfer surface to proactive transfer situations.

When we are interested in discovering and applying general principles to the problems of transfer, it is discouraging to find that research has produced such conflicting results. But we should not be surprised at such results when we consider the complicated nature of transfer, the great number of variables that may be involved in transfer, and the various kinds of transfer problem that have been investigated. Many studies of transfer differ so greatly from one another that few direct comparisons can be made between them. As we have noted, some employ proactive designs, others employ retroactive designs. In some studies, transfer has meant the "transplanting" of a response acquired in one situation to some other situation; other studies have aimed at determining whether learning a new response is facilitated or interfered with by some previous experience. There have also been differences in the nature of the responses that have been investigated. Many studies have explored the transfer of verbal learning; others have considered transfer from one psychomotor task to another; and still others have studied transfer effects from verbal to motor tasks. Some transfer studies have made use of simple verbal or manipulative tasks; others have employed highly abstract and complicated problems.

So it is not surprising that research on transfer presents a complex and often confusing picture. It is possible that there is no single model or set of principles applicable to all transfer situations. At least, we do not seem to have accumulated sufficient information on all aspects of transfer to provide a basis for broadly applicable generalizations. Certainly, for the teacher attempting to ensure the greatest amount of transfer of material being taught in the classroom, there is no simple, unfailing set of rules to follow.

GENERALIZATION AND DISCRIMINATION IN TRANSFER

Despite the complexities of transfer, there are two elements common to all transfer situations: *generalization* and *discrimination.* Since we are only infrequently called upon to respond to a pattern of stimulation that is identical from one situation to another, some degree of generalization must occur if transfer is to take place. We must respond as though the two situations were essentially equivalent; but we must also discover to what extent or in what ways the two situations can differ without calling for a different response. This is simply another way of stating that we must make certain discriminations if we are to detect critical similarities between the two situations and if we are to avoid faulty generalizations (negative transfer).

If a child learns the name of a particular bird from an illustration in a book, he may identify the bird correctly when it appears at a bird feeder even though the illustration did not reproduce the bird's colors with complete accuracy and was smaller than the bird's actual size. He makes the same recognition response to the bird that he has made to the illustration—that is, positive transfer has occurred—although the two patterns of stimulation, though similar in some respects, were not identical.

Similarities between transfer and concept formation are rather apparent, since both require generalization and discrimination. Concept formation, as a matter of fact, is a special case of transfer. When we learn to respond to some general category of stimulus events on the basis of our experience with only certain members of that category, we do so on the basis of transfer. The child who makes the response "dog" to all the dogs he encounters, although his experiences have been limited to a few neighborhood dogs or to some pictures of dogs, is demonstrating the effects of transfer from these experiences.

If we fail to make the necessary discriminations, however, faulty generalizations can lead to negative transfer. A child noting that the double-*e* combination in words such as "need" produces a long vowel sound may attempt to spell "show" with a double *o* rather than with *ow*. Negative transfer is most likely to arise when some elements in the stimulus situation remain constant while others change and a new response is required. The learner fails to discriminate the changed elements and generalizes from those that remain constant. The student in an introductory statistics course, confronted with the question "Which is greater: a difference significant at the 1-percent level or one significant at the 10-percent level?" may be strongly inclined, on the basis of previous experiences, to respond, incorrectly, "At the 10-percent level."

While generalization is essential to transfer, it must be brought under the learner's control. One approach is through practice in making discriminations. Harlow found that when monkeys had experience with a variety of discrimination tasks their ability to solve new problems improved markedly.[4] In other words, there was a positive transfer effect from this experience. Monkeys that had learned that a grape would always be found under the larger of two containers were presented with another problem in which the grape would be found under a pyramidal rather than a cylindrical container. (The relative size of the two containers was irrelevant.) As might be anticipated, initially there was negative transfer from one task to another. However, as the tasks continued to be changed and the monkeys were required to respond not only to size or shape but to the color or position of the containers, they became more and more adept at solving successive problems.

---

4. H. Harlow, "The Formation of Learning Sets," *Psychological Review* (January 1949), pp. 51–65.

We can view these results in several ways. We can say that these animals "learned how to learn." But it is more helpful to note that their original tendency toward stimulus generalization from one problem to the next was eliminated, or at least brought under control, when they repeatedly found that it did not lead them to a quick solution. On the other hand, it would seem that they acquired one useful generalization as a result of these varied experiences: They learned that a discrimination—that is, a choice—had to be made and that this choice had to be changed if, initially, it proved incorrect. They had gone beyond the stage where they associated a particular color or shape with reinforcement and had acquired a principle that they could apply to other problem situations.

Some of our educational procedures are directed toward this same end. Teaching rules of spelling, principles of mathematics, or fundamentals of English is, whether we recognize it or not, a means of providing students with a basis for generalization and transfer. The rule or principle helps to bring our tendency to generalize under some degree of control, with a consequent increase in the probability that positive transfer will occur.

VARIABLES IN TRANSFER

If generalization and discrimination are central to transfer, those variables that affect generalization and discrimination should influence the nature and extent of transfer. Some of the more important of these variables are:

Predifferentiation. What happens when we describe, verbally, to a beginning swimmer or bicycle rider the motor responses we wish him to make? Or when music teachers use such terms as "soaring" or "spritely," with their physical connotations, to describe the emotional reactions they wish their students to experience when they hear a particular musical composition? In mathematics, the physical sciences, and the social sciences, we frequently use graphs, models, and diagrams to help students who are trying to deal with essentially symbolic problems. Are such procedures effective? Can we really teach a motor skill by means of verbal instruction? Do responses learned in connection with problems presented visually transfer to similar problems presented verbally?

In many situations, a few minutes of verbal explanation may appreciably shorten the time needed to acquire a psychomotor skill; some manipulative practice or a visual experience may hasten the solution of a symbolic problem. Positive transfer can occur even though the first task involves no specific experience with either the stimuli or the responses of the second task. The psychologist may be intrigued with the question of how such transfer can occur, but, for the teacher there are other important questions: How much verbal explanation is desirable in teaching a motor skill? At what point should it be introduced? How can models be used in teaching abstract concepts without misleading the learner and causing him to fixate on concrete aspects of the model?

Whether or not positive transfer will occur depends on the extent to which the initial learning results in predifferentiation of stimuli. If such predifferentiation occurs, transfer effects are possible even though the two learning tasks are dissimilar—for example, verbal and psychomotor. The central task of the learner is to differentiate, to discover the critical aspects of stimulus patterns. A model may focus his attention on the significant elements in some abstract problem; verbal instructions may direct his attention to the kinesthetic sensations that will serve as cues in acquiring some motor skill. If verbal instructions or the use of models and illustrations result in positive transfer, it is probably because they produce a predifferentiation of the stimuli in the second task. Gagné and Baker,[5] for example, presented subjects with a task requiring them to watch a board containing a large number of lights, each with its own switch. When one of the lights flashed on, the subjects were to turn it off as quickly as possible by throwing the correct switch. Subjects who had previously been given an opportunity to label the lights with letters of the alphabet were found to have a marked advantage later in learning to associate lights with switches.

Research has also indicated that transfer from verbal pretraining to motor skills is greatest when the motor elements of the task are relatively simple and that transfer decreases as the motor elements become more complex. Apparently, as the task becomes more complicated, verbal pretraining becomes less helpful in preparing the learner for the discriminations he must make. This

---

5. R. M. Gagné and K. E. Baker, "Stimulus Predifferentiation as a Factor in Transfer of Training," *Journal of Experimental Psychology* (August 1950), pp. 439–51.

suggests that, in teaching complex motor tasks, less transfer can be expected from verbal directions and proportionately more time should be spent in actual practice. It is also possible that, in the case of some complex motor tasks, practice may be necessary to make the verbal instructions meaningful. Here the greatest transfer may result from spacing verbal instructions throughout the learning sequence.

Organization and Level of Learning. Other things being equal, highly organized, thoroughly learned responses show greater positive transfer than responses that are poorly organized and indifferently learned. Transfer, as we have noted, is impossible without retention. Organization and overlearning increase transfer for the same reasons that they increase retention: critical stimuli become more sharply discriminated, and competition among responses is reduced. Highly organized material, such as concepts and principles, since they are applicable in a variety of circumstances, can be expected to have greater transfer value than responses that are appropriate only in a specific situation.

When subjects are required to learn to make an old response to a new stimulus, overlearning produces an increase in positive transfer. Learning a new response to an old stimulus ordinarily gives rise to negative transfer, and continued practice on the first task initially results in an increase in the amount of negative transfer. However, if we continue to practice the first task, negative transfer effects usually decline to zero. This indicates that competition between old and new responses has been reduced by overlearning. An inexperienced driver, for example, often becomes confused and responds poorly when he tries to drive an unfamiliar car that requires him to make new braking, steering, or gear-shifting responses. An experienced driver, however, although he may have driven another car with quite different controls and handling characteristics for a number of years, adapts quickly to driving the new vehicle with little or no negative transfer from his previous driving habits.

Task Difficulty. A common teaching tactic is to train the learner on a simplified form of some task, with the expectation or the hope that positive transfer to a more difficult version of the task will occur. Rarely do we train students on complex tasks in order to promote positive transfer to simpler tasks. Ordinarily, it makes good sense to practice the simpler task first, and some positive transfer usually does occur, but there are more ramifications than many teachers assume.

Frequently, the more difficult task contains all the elements of the easier task, while the easier task includes only some of the components of the difficult task. In such cases there may be greater transfer if the student does his initial learning on the more complex task—provided, of course, he is capable of learning it. Not only does he learn to perform the more difficult task, but, as some studies have indicated, transfer from the difficult to the easy task may be equivalent to direct practice on the easy task.

Some tasks, however, require the learner first to identify the stimuli to which he should respond. In such cases, preliminary training on a simplified version may produce the greatest positive transfer, since it permits the learner to discover more readily what discriminations he must make. If the learner attempts his initial learning on the complex task, the necessary discriminations may be so numerous or require such fine distinctions that he fails to identify them. In such situations, initial training on easy tasks will result in greater transfer than initial training on difficult tasks. But note that transfer is not automatically and invariably greater if we go from the simpler task to the more difficult one. If we wish to increase the possibility of positive transfer, it makes good sense to analyze the tasks in terms of the demands that are being made on the learner and then to plan instruction accordingly.

Ability of the Learner. It is a common observation that brighter students show greater positive transfer from one experience to another than do less intelligent students. Unfortunately, this tells us more about the nature of intelligence and intelligence tests than it does about transfer.

Psychologists who construct intelligence tests must try somehow to eliminate or equate the effects of experience on test performance. Since it is impossible, practically, to construct items whose solutions will be entirely unaffected by the experiences of those who take the test, questions are usually based on some background of experience that is presumably common to all testees. One rarely stated but implicit assumption is that the greater ability of the more intelligent testees to profit from their experiences will be reflected in their superior test performance. It is not surprising, therefore, to find that intelligence-test scores and performance in transfer situations are positively related. Since intelligence tests are designed to measure the effects of prior experience, essentially the same factors are being measured in both cases. The many studies that have reported a positive relationship between transfer and intelligence are merely indicating that people who do well on one measure of transfer—intelligence tests—perform well on other transfer tasks.

THE NATURE OF TRANSFER: A REAPPRAISAL

Some investigations in recent years, though not aimed directly at the question of transfer, have given rise to a reconsideration of its nature. Research on learning sets has suggested that a general transfer effect may result from specific but varied experiences. Harlow's monkeys, as a result of their experiences with a variety of tasks, became, in general, better problem solvers. One might say that they became more flexible and mentally agile in their approach to new problems. Recently, R. W. Gerard wrote:

> As a lifelong student of the brain and of behavior I am keenly aware of the great capacity of the brain to learn and to learn to learn, and of the rather rapid decrease in these high potencies from infancy onward. Baby chimpanzees (or humans) denied the experience of patterned vision during the early months of life may never achieve the effective discrimination of patterns . . . . Rats given rich experiences during growth show a thicker brain cortex than those deprived of such experience. In general, functioning increases the ability to function, in the intellectual realm as in the physical one: exercising the brain is as productive as exercising the muscles and the cardio-vascular system.[6]

This sounds remarkably like the doctrine of mental discipline. Is it possible that we have been hasty in rejecting this view of transfer and in accepting the theory of identical elements? It seems more likely that we have taken an oversimplified view of the nature of transfer and have interpreted "identity" too narrowly in considering the question of what constitutes identical elements in two situations.

---

6. R. W. Gerard, "Intelligence, Information and Education," *Science* (May 1965), pp. 762–65.

There is no question that transfer can and often does occur when learners recognize similarities between either stimuli or responses. But identical elements need not always be specific symbols or actions. A person who has learned one foreign language often finds that he can learn a second foreign language much more readily, even though, linguistically, the two languages may be unrelated to one another. Since there are no common elements of vocabulary or syntax, how can we account for this transfer effect? Learning the second language is also a situation that calls for a certain routine of study, for changes in one's accustomed patterns of thought, and for a willingness to attempt unfamiliar vocalizations. In this sense, the two tasks do have common elements, even though they do not share common verbal stimuli and responses.

Material taught on a rote basis, with emphasis on its application only to a specific situation, may not transfer readily to other situations, even though both situations include some identical elements. When geometry, for example, is taught as a process of memorizing theorems and proofs, it is not surprising that students show no greater tendency toward logical behavior in other areas than do students who have never studied geometry. As a matter of fact, they will probably not even show improved ability to memorize other materials. Research indicates, however, that positive transfer is likely to occur when the initial learning stresses principles or generalizable techniques. As studies of high-school students have demonstrated, geometry courses taught with an emphasis on critical reasoning do improve ability to transfer syllogistic reasoning to nongeometric problems.[7]

Finally, as Gerard has pointed out, organisms raised in intellectually stimulating environments exhibit differences in the physiology of the central nervous system and generally demonstrate superior learning performance.[8] For example, children raised in institutions, where they receive scant personal attention, or in slums, remote mountain settlements, or other environments lacking in intellectual stimulation generally do not perform as well on intellectually demanding tasks as do children who have had more challenging and varied experiences. The person who is alert and

---

7. Gilbert Ulmer, "Some Suggestions for Teaching Geometry to Develop Clear Thinking," *Kansas University Studies in Education* (Lawrence, Kans.: University of Kansas, 1942), Vol. II, No. 7.
8. Gerard, *op. cit.*

responsive to his environment is probably better able to make the discriminations essential to transfer and, having had experience with a variety of discrimination tasks, has had an opportunity to develop the necessary control over the tendency to generalize.

The factors that influence transfer, and transfer effects themselves, quite possibly are distributed along a continuum from the highly specific to the very general. At one extreme, we have transfer resulting from such specific elements as common items of vocabulary, identical mathematical symbols, and specific motor responses. But somewhere along this continuum we note that transfer may also occur when the learner recognizes and makes use of some general principle or when habits of study, attitudes toward difficult material, or feelings about one's capabilities and chances of success or failure affect subsequent learning. At the other extreme, we have the possibility that the varied experiences provided over an extended period of time by a stimulating environment may result in a generally improved ability to use the results of previous experience in new situations.

TRANSFER AND TEACHING

It is not difficult to present a plausible case for the broad transfer value of a generally stimulating environment or a liberal education —possibly because we are not usually required to furnish specific evidence. However, many training programs and many of our educational objectives call for specific transfer effects. We want to train drivers who will exhibit certain definite competencies when they are on our highways. We want to know if a particular instructional program will produce skilled medical technicians or effective public-school teachers. What do we actually know about the facilitation of transfer in such situations?

Although the concept of transfer is fundamental to every educational program, our efforts frequently result in much less positive transfer than we would wish, and often they result in negative transfer. Some modest increase in the amount of positive transfer is possible, however, if we deliberately plan for transfer. Teachers can, for example, try to provide enough overlearning to ensure retention and to prevent confusion and negative transfer. Overlearning need not be synonymous with repetitive practice or rote drill. If the experiences required for such overlearning are sufficiently varied, not only can the teacher avoid monotony and boredom, but practice in discrimination can be provided and an opportunity created for voluntarily learning to vary generalizations. One means of providing variation in experience is through class discussions in which ideas may be presented in a variety of contexts.

Since highly organized material and, in particular, generalizations, or unifying concepts, and principles have greater potential for transfer than do isolated bits of learning, instruction that emphasizes such learning can be expected to show increased transfer. There is some evidence, moreover, that principles discovered or derived independently by the learner are more transferable than those given to him. Teachers, however, have a particular problem in trying to teach general principles to very young children and slow learners. General principles tend to be abstract; since these children lack the ability of older or more intelligent children to grasp abstractions, the teacher might be better advised to give them the principle in the form of a rule and show them specifically where and how to apply it. Although these children may require a great deal of practice in order to learn, we are probably mistaken in assuming that this practice must be highly repetitive if transfer is to occur. We acknowledge the short attention span of young and retarded children but apparently ignore the need for variation in learning experiences that this implies.

Fundamentally, the most useful but perhaps the most difficult thing the teacher can do to facilitate transfer is to try to analyze the transfer task in terms of the problems it presents *to the learner*. Too frequently we organize and present material in a manner that is logical and consistent to the *teacher*—that is, *to someone who has already learned*—without really considering how learners learn. One of the most important contributions to education of programed instruction has been that it has directed our attention to the obvious: that most human learning is sequential and is built upon transfer from previous learning. When we try to answer the question "What does the learner need to know in order to take the next step in this learning sequence?" we are addressing ourselves to the problem of effective transfer.

This approach has been studied experimentally by Robert Gagné.[9] Starting with some *terminal behavior* that the learner

9. R. M. Gagné, "The Acquisition of Knowledge," *Psychological Review* (July 1962), pp. 355–65.

is to acquire, he has attempted to work back to the next set of behaviors that are presumed to be necessary prerequisites for acquiring the terminal behavior. The acquisition of these behaviors is, in turn, based upon the acquisition of behaviors of a still lower order. By working backwards in this way, we reach the point where the learner already possesses the necessary behaviors and this becomes the beginning point for instruction. The result is not a logical sequence of subject matter but a psychological sequence of learning stages, or a learning structure. Gagné contends that generalizations, or learning sets, acquired at each step in this structure transfer and facilitate learning the next step. This explanation is supported by the fact that he found those groups who were given a variety of examples had learned significantly more than those groups who were given a narrow range of examples.

Ausubel has experimented with what he refers to as *advance organizers* [10]—concepts and generalizations into which subsequent learning could be assimilated. In one study, the experimental group was given material about alloys and metals and a set of concepts that could be used to organize information about alloys. The control group was presented with an historical introduction to metallurgy designed to arouse interest. When both groups were given information about the metallurgy of steel, the experimental group showed significantly greater learning and retention. Other experiments by Ausubel [11] have consistently shown an advantage for groups using advance organizers.

Ausubel and Gagné have devised no rules for creating advance organizers or for constructing hierarchies of learning sets. But there is no reason that teachers cannot familiarize themselves with this research and proceed in the same pragmatic manner to develop their own advance organizers and instructional strategies.

Gagné has suggested that we should distinguish between *vertical transfer,* as implied in his learning structures, and *lateral transfer.* The latter type Gagné describes as "a kind of generalizing that

---

10. D. P. Ausubel, "The Use of Advance Organizers in the Learning and Retention of Meaningful Verbal Material," *Journal of Educational Psychology* (October 1960), pp. 267–72.
11. D. P. Ausubel and D. Fitzgerald, "Organizer, General Background and Antecedent Learning Variables in Sequential Verbal Learning," *Journal of Educational Psychology* (December 1962), pp. 243–49, and D. P. Ausubel and M. Youssef, "Role of Discriminability in Meaningful Parallel Learning," *Journal of Educational Psychology* (December 1963), pp. 331–36.

spreads over a broad set of situations at roughly the same 'level of complexity.' "[12]

From the viewpoint of the teacher, this distinction could be an important one if, as Gagné contends, different conditions are necessary for the two types of transfer. The conditions for vertical transfer are both internal and external. *Internal* conditions are mastery by the student of the relevant lower-order capabilities and the acquisition of a variety of previous knowledge. The *external* conditions are the structure of the learning task and the directions given to the learner to stimulate his recall and to guide his activities.

The most important conditions for lateral transfer, according to Gagné, are probably *internal* to the individual. Breadth of knowledge is obviously necessary for lateral transfer, but some students just seem more able than others to relate their knowledge to a wider variety of situations. Some of these differences in lateral-transfer ability may stem from innate factors, but students' ability to achieve lateral transfer undoubtedly can be improved through practice in applying their capabilities in a wide variety of circumstances.

The factors affecting transfer are so many and so complex that we may be inclined to throw up our hands, go on with our teaching, and hope for the best. This is precisely what we should *not* do, and it is one of the reasons we are not more successful in increasing the amount of transfer of school subjects. Clearly, our ability to control the complicated forces affecting transfer is sharply limited. In most cases, transfer is largely a matter of guesswork and chance. But, as the preceding suggestion indicates, there are some things we can do. Even a small increase, as Thorndike pointed out, can be very important:

> Finally, it must be remembered that a very small spread of training may be of great educational value if it extends over a wide enough field. If a hundred hours of training on being scientific about chemistry produced only one-hundredth as much improvement in being scientific about all sorts of facts, it would yet be a very remunerative educational force.[13]

---

12. R. M. Gagné, *The Conditions of Learning* (New York: Holt, Rinehart and Winston, 1965), p. 231.
13. E. L. Thorndike, *Educational Psychology* (New York: Teachers College, Columbia University Press, 1913), p. 421.

A second reason we are not more successful in promoting transfer is that we tend to assume that learning will naturally and automatically transfer—that it should be obvious to students that a particular response is generalizable to other situations. But, as Allport has noted: "Time and again it appears that identical elements in themselves have no power to effect transfer. Only when a general principle is understood as applicable to two or more fields does the training in one carry over to the others." [14]

Teachers must deliberately provide for transfer. One way of doing this is to point out to students that they should expect their knowledge to transfer and, wherever possible, to indicate potential transfer situations. Keeping alert for opportunities to apply one's knowledge can become as well established as any other habit. Sometimes, however, we teach as though some particular knowledge or skill were an end in itself and transfer a completely irrelevant consideration. The teacher must remind himself to think beyond the immediate lesson, the course, and the classroom.

Suggestions for Class Discussion and Further Investigation

1. It has often been stated by educators that young children are naturally creative and original until this characteristic is eliminated by adults. From what you know about lateral transfer does this statement make sense?
2. Is it possible that a child's readiness to move on to higher grade levels and to other subjects may be a matter of maturation as well as a function of transfer of learning? How would you distinguish between maturation and transfer?
3. What factors would you consider in determining whether or not a child is ready for first grade? For learning to read?
4. For the student who does not go on to college, are there any possible positive transfer effects from studying algebra?
5. Is the lack of scholastic success of culturally disadvantaged children due to negative transfer or a lack of positive transfer? What difference does your answer make in terms of assisting these children?

---

14. Gordon Allport, *Personality: a Psychological Interpretation* (New York: Holt, Rinehart and Winston, 1937), p. 277.

6. Teachers are often urged to "teach for transfer." Is it always possible to do so?
8. Students who are completely honest insofar as their friends' money or personal belongings are concerned sometimes cheat on examinations or copy homework. Is this a problem in transfer of learning?

Suggestions for Further Reading

H. Ellis, *The Transfer of Learning* (New York: Macmillan, 1965) provides a good, up-to-date coverage of this topic. The book as a whole may go somewhat beyond the interests of teachers, but the first eighty-five pages are of particular value.

A concise review of the literature on transfer, up to 1958, with emphasis on transfer and school practices, is offered in J. M. Stephens, "Transfer of Learning," *Encyclopedia of Educational Research,* 3rd ed. (New York: Macmillan, 1960), pp. 1535–43.

Two texts on human learning that contain clear discussions and interpretations of the major experimental investigations of transfer are: James Deese, *The Psychology of Learning,* 2nd ed. (New York: McGraw-Hill, 1958), pp. 213–35; and B. R. Bugelski, *The Psychology of Learning* (New York: Holt, Rinehart and Winston, 1956), pp. 382–416.

For the student interested in reading original-research studies on transfer, an excellent paperback is available: R. F. Grose and R. C. Binney, eds., *Transfer of Learning, an Enduring Problem in Psychology* (Princeton, N.J.: Van Nostrand, 1963).

Because transfer has such a pervasive effect upon all aspects of learning, studies of transfer that may be of interest to teachers can be found under a wide variety of headings. Among the more likely topics for investigation are: verbal behavior, retention, concept formation, and problem solving. *The Journal of Educational Psychology* and the December issues of *Psychological Abstracts* are particularly good sources.

Chapter Eight

Complex Behavior: Skills and Problem Solving

In the preceding chapters, we have been concerned less with the nature of the responses learned than with the characteristics of learning itself and with the variables that affect learning. The exceptions were verbal behavior and concept formation, and even here, for purposes of clarity, we considered relatively simple responses. But human behavior is not simple. We operate and repair complicated machinery, teach classes, perform involved computations, play intricate games, and seek solutions to difficult problems. These complex behaviors can be classified under two general headings: *skilled performances* and *problem solving.*

If we define a skilled performance as something done exceedingly well or with great proficiency, it is impossible to distinguish between skills and problem solving. The accomplished skier and the student who turns in a flawless translation would both be considered skilled by such a definition, although most of us would have a feeling that there are important differences between the two performances.

Psychologists usually use the term *skill* only when they are referring to some complex psychomotor activity, such as walking, driving a car, or catching a ball. They apply the term *problem solving* to tasks that require the learner to apply some principle in selecting from among a number of possible responses those that will lead to a desired goal.

By defining skills and problem solving in this fashion, we can make some distinctions between the two. Clearly, learning to ride a bicycle and learning to solve a problem in geometry present the learner with quite different tasks. But perhaps such differences are *too* obvious. Because learning is an inferred process, we see only the behavioral changes that are associated with it. The changes that result from the acquisition of a motor skill are often so clearly different from changes in problem-solving behavior that we are likely to overlook some of the similarities and underlying common elements. When we compare riding a bicycle with proving a geometric theorem, we see only that they are two very different forms of behavior.

But both skills and problem solving require the learner to make discriminations. He must learn what to look for, how to make critical distinctions, and how to identify important cues. Both require cognitive activity. In problem solving, understanding the nature of the task is of critical importance, and in many problem situations success in achieving a solution depends on the ability to use abstract concepts. The importance of cognitive factors may be less apparent in the learning of skills, since we tend to focus on the motor aspects of the task. But it is significant that tests of intelligence and of specialized knowledge have been used successfully to predict the rates at which individuals will learn during the early stages of acquiring a skill.

In some instances, it may be very difficult to distinguish clearly between learning skills and learning to solve problems. Some skills, in fact, include many of the elements of problem solving. Driving an automobile, for example, requires a high level of perceptual and motor skill, but it also requires a knowledge of how and when to change lanes and some understanding of the effects of centrifugal force. The tennis player's skilled performance is, in part, the result of his ability to solve a series of problems calling for judgment, decision making, and strategy. The teacher engaged in a skilled performance known as "teaching a class" is also solving a series of problems: selecting the best means of clarifying a concept, deciding when to explain and when to question, choosing from among many possible examples the one that will best demonstrate a principle.

Our ability to solve some problems and the manner in which we solve them may also depend on whether or not we possess certain skills. For example, the problem of obtaining objects that are out of reach is eventually solved by most young children partly through learning the skills of walking and climbing. And the skills we possess may affect the ways in which we go about solving certain problems. The athletic adolescent and his poorly coordinated classmate are likely to arrive at quite different solutions to the problem of obtaining the attention and approval of their peers.

Sometimes we distinguish between skills and problem solving by making value judgments about the relative importance of the two. We tend to regard the acquisition of skills as a "lower" form of learning than problem solving. It is true that one of the ways in which man is most clearly superior to other forms of life is in his ability to solve problems. It is also true that some individuals of limited intelligence do become highly skilled athletes or performers. But these facts should not cause us to underrate the importance of skills in human behavior. During most of our waking hours we are engaged in some form of skilled activity. We button clothes, manipulate a wide variety of utensils, walk, drive automobiles, turn pages of books, and type. The skills we have acquired enable us to move easily and efficiently through a complex physical environment. They enable us to carry on routine tasks while attending to other concerns. They are often the means by which we achieve other important ends; and the skills we use in our hobbies and sports add greatly to our enjoyment of life. The ability to perform skillfully and the ability to solve problems supplement rather than compete with one another.

SKILLS

The principal characteristics that distinguish skill performances from other forms of complex behavior are *manipulation* (or *movement responses*), *coordination, response to perceptual and proprioceptive stimuli,* and *automation.*

While manipulation and movement are characteristics of all skills, in some skills, such as walking, swimming, and diving, only the performer's own body is manipulated. Riding a bicycle, playing baseball, buttoning a shirt, and driving a car, however, require that other objects as well be manipulated.

Simple reflexes, such as blinking an eyelid or withdrawing one's hand from a hot object, are not skills, because they are not coordinated responses. That is, they do not require the integration of simpler responses into complex performances. Although we speak of "sailing a boat," "typing," or "playing the clarinet," we should not be misled into thinking of these skills as unitary responses. Pressing down a brake or clutch pedal, shifting gears, and turning a steering wheel are each relatively simple responses that almost anyone can perform. But only the skillful driver can integrate them into a smoothly coordinated act.

One of the most distinctive aspects of skilled behavior is the extent to which it is continuously guided by information being received by the performer. The performer receives this information either as input or as feedback. *Input* can take the form of directions that are given to the person ("Push the red button" or "Turn the wheel slightly to the left") or as perceptual cues (the trajectory of a ball or the estimated distance of the car from the curb). *Feedback* is analogous to the concept of reinforcement in other forms of learning. It is information the individual receives as a consequence of his own responses. In some cases the immediate source of the feedback is external: he turns the wheel and sees the car move to one side, or he shifts improperly and hears the clash of gears. But some feedback comes from proprioceptive cues—that is, from sensations arising from forces and pressures within the performer's own body. As we become skilled, we learn how it "feels," for example, when we are controlling a racquet properly or driving well.

Not only are the responses of the skilled driver smoothly coordinated, but, with the achievement of a high level of skill, he becomes increasingly unaware of both the specific responses he is making and the cues to which he is responding. He shifts gears, steers, and regulates his speed while giving most of his attention, not to these individual acts, but to the road and the movements of other cars. William James and other early psychologists applied the term *automation* to this characteristic of skills. During automation, skills become increasingly resistant to stress and interference from other stimuli. We apparently rely increasingly on input and feedback and less on cognitive direction, so long as the situation in which we are performing remains stable and we continue to receive information indicating that we are making appropriate responses.

Paul Fitts has suggested that we might regard the skilled performer as operating at two levels.[1] At one level he is engaged in a repetitive pattern of relatively simple responses or in an integrated series of such subroutines that function more or less autonomously. But, at a second level, this autonomous behavior can be interrupted, altered, and controlled by the performer. When we walk, for example, we usually pay little attention to

---

1. Paul M. Fitts, "Perceptual-Motor Skill Learning," in A. W. Melton, ed., *Categories of Human Learning* (New York: Academic Press, 1964), pp. 244–83.

the act of walking itself, and we exert little or no conscious control over the manner in which we walk. But, if we are suddenly confronted by some obstacle or a change in the gradient of the path, this new information causes us to change our pattern of walking. We step higher, or stop short, or perhaps increase our stride.

The Learning of Skill Performances. Simply describing the characteristics of a skill tells us something, but not everything, about the task confronting someone who wants to learn the skill. Before the highly integrated response patterns of a skill emerge, what must we learn?

Fitts has proposed that learning a complex skill progresses through three stages: the *cognitive phase,* the *fixation phase,* and the *autonomous phase.*[2]

Cognitive phase. The cognitive aspects of some skills are very apparent. In driving an automobile or participating in games such as football or tennis, certain information and a knowledge of relevant strategies and principles are essential to a skilled performance. The importance of cognitive learning varies, of course, with the particular skill to be acquired. It is less important in swimming or skiing, for example, than in typing or playing a musical instrument.

However, cognitive factors play an important role even in the learning of the manipulative aspects of skills. In teaching the motor and perceptual elements of a task, instructors often try to describe and analyze the task for the learner. Research indicates that such procedures can be very helpful in assisting the learner to discriminate between relevant and irrelevant cues and in alerting him to possible sources of error. In an experiment at the University of Illinois Aviation Psychology Laboratory, instructors found that the amount of training prior to soloing could be cut approximately in half by training procedures that stressed verbal instruction during performance, establishing appropriate expectancies, "talking through" maneuvers, and "intellectualizing" the tasks.[3]

---

2. Paul M. Fitts, "Factors in Complex Learning," in Robert Glaser, ed., *Training Research and Education* (New York: Wiley, 1965).
3. R. E. Flexman, W. G. Matheny, and E. L. Brown, "Evaluation of the School Link and Special Methods of Instruction," *University of Illinois Bulletin* (July 1950).

Fixation phase. The cognitive phase of skill learning is followed by a phase in which the manipulative responses are practiced and improved upon and finally become established well enough that we can perform the act without an excessive number of errors.

Complex performances require us to develop skill in a number of independent or semi-independent behavior sequences that we must then put together into a coordinated performance. During the early stages of the fixation phase we concentrate on learning these subroutines. We practice shifting gears and regulating the flow of gas by means of the accelerator, or we practice depressing the space bar on the typewriter with our right thumb and throwing the carriage return with our left hand. During the later stages of the fixation phase we practice putting these responses together as part of an integrated pattern.

It is difficult to distinguish sharply between the fixation phase and the cognitive phase, for the learner may reach a point in his practice where further progress depends on additional cognitive learning. Early studies on learning to type,[4] for example, indicated that learners reach plateaus in their performance and that their ability to move to higher levels of proficiency depends on cognitive and motivational factors rather than simply on increased manipulative ability. The beginning typist tends to type letter by letter or, at best, word by word. Unless he is strongly motivated to move to a phrase by phrase level and is able to read and retain entire phrases, he makes little further progress.

Autonomous phase. As the learner becomes more skilled, as his responses become better coordinated, he gradually moves into the autonomous phase where responses require less and less conscious direction.

Reaching the autonomous stage is usually a slow process. To move from the fixation to the autonomous phase, he must greatly overlearn the response patterns. Most instructional procedures, however, end at the fixation phase, at the point where the responses have been reasonably well established and errors have been reduced to an acceptable level. Most of us, once we can type thirty words a minute, drive well enough to avoid accidents under normal conditions, or swim well enough to feel fairly safe in the water,

4. William F. Book, *The Psychology of Skill,* University of Montana Publications in Psychology, Bulletin 53, Psychological Series No. 1 (1908), pp. 7–100.

stop taking instructions and discontinue any serious practice. This is probably unfortunate, since skill performances at this stage are still susceptible to the effects of distraction, fatigue, boredom, and interference from competing responses. Research indicates that improvement may continue over a very long period of time but does tend to come more and more slowly. Teachers should anticipate that the less highly motivated learners may content themselves with the thought that they can "do it well enough" long before they reach the autonomous phase.

Achievement of the autonomous phase of a skill does not mean that the performer begins to operate in a machinelike manner, uninfluenced by any external cues. On the contrary, he is probably making more precise discriminations and responding to cues more quickly and accurately. The beginning driver, for example, may allow the car to stray over the center line or onto the shoulder of the road before he makes the necessary corrections. The skilled driver, however, responds quickly and deftly to minimal perceptual cues and to proprioceptive feedback, correcting slight deviations almost as soon as they occur. Moreover, he is more likely to respond only to relevant cues. The conversations of other occupants of the car or even a sudden emergency do not disrupt his well-established driving habits.

Demonstration and Guidance in the Acquisition of Skills. Probably the most common technique in teaching skills is the demonstration; someone who is already competent in the skill performs for the benefit of the learner. For many learners this procedure may have some motivational value. It may cause the beginner to aspire to the expert's level of competence—if he is not discouraged by the gap between his own level of performance and that of the expert. But, unfortunately, a demonstration by a skilled performer may illustrate only the autonomous phase of the skill or the latter stages of the fixation phase. This performance may clarify for the learner what he must ultimately be able to do, but it tells him little about the simpler responses or subroutines that make up the final act. The instructor is more likely to be effective if he is able to break the skill down into its component parts, demonstrate each of them, and then guide the learner through these subroutines. However, if the instructor himself has reached the autonomous stage, this may be difficult for him to do. He may be unaware of all the external cues to which he is responding and unable to describe the sensations that serve as proprioceptive cues.

Even the most carefully analyzed demonstration cannot tell the learner how each of the components of a skilled performance are integrated into the final performance. This is something that requires direct experience, preferably with some guidance. The instructor may guide the learner verbally, by pointing out cues and correct responses. Or he may actually manipulate the learner through the act, placing his hands in the proper position, correcting his posture, or helping him grasp the pencil or racquet properly.

One purpose of such guidance is to familiarize the learner with the nature of the task and with cues, both external and proprioceptive, to which he must respond. Some instructors attempt to provide this experience indirectly by asking the learner to imagine that he is performing the skill or by requiring him to describe each step in the activity. This type of practice is probably better than no practice at all, but proprioceptive cues are so important in skill performance that guidance procedures that provide for the active participation of the learner are generally superior.

Well-planned instruction, including guidance and demonstration, during the cognitive and fixation phases of learning a skill can help the learner avoid making and practicing errors. Instruction can also reduce greatly the amount of time and practice needed to learn a skill. Unfortunately, we tend to mass our demonstrations and guidance at the beginning of instruction, and some of this information may be useful to the learner only after he has attempted to perform the skill. Guidance and demonstration, ideally, should come at those points where the learner can best use them. This means that the teacher must assess the learner's level of skill acquisition and try to determine what information and how much of it he needs. Too little direction may restrict the learner; too much may confuse and frustrate him.

Practice and the Learning of Skills. "Practice makes perfect," we are often told. But practice can also make imperfect, since incorrect responses as well as correct responses can be established by practice. Moreover, practice without reinforcement may lead to the extinction of a response rather than to its improvement.

A great deal has been written about the relative merits of massed versus distributed practice, active versus passive practice, practice by wholes versus practice by parts, and practice for accuracy versus practice for speed. And much of what has been written consists of generalizations that need qualification. First, most of the statements about practice are statements about relative rather than absolute states of affairs. A routine of twenty-minute work periods with ten-minute rest intervals would be considered distributed practice if we compared it with an unbroken sixty-minute work period. However, if we compare it with a distribution of ten-minute work periods alternated with five minutes of rest, we might consider it massed practice. Similarly, although some practice procedures produce more learner participation than others, it is probably impossible for a learner to practice in any manner and be completely passive. Whether practicing by wholes is superior or inferior to practicing by parts depends to some extent on the complexity and length of the whole task. And practice for sheer speed, with no attempt to achieve accuracy, is perhaps closer to random behavior than to practice.

How can we judge the relative merits of practice procedures? First, we must decide what, in general, we are trying to accomplish through practice. Practice often serves more than one purpose. It gives the learner experience with the cues he must use to guide his responses. Such experience is particularly important in learning to respond to proprioceptive cues, since the instructor usually cannot describe these cues accurately to the learner. Practice also provides the learner with feedback that serves to reinforce correct responses and enables him to judge the adequacy of his responses.

How long should practice periods be? There is no simple answer to this question, but the teacher can be guided by some of the considerations mentioned above. Ideally, practice sessions should be long enough to permit the maximum amount of practice without creating fatigue, boredom, and a rise in error rate. A marked increase in the learner's error rate probably indicates that a rest period is called for. Some skill performances call for a fairly long "warm-up" period. If practice sessions are too short, the learner may not have a chance to reach his maximum performance before the practice period ends.

In general, practice sessions should be long enough for the complete act to be practiced several times. Practicing by parts, particularly when the task is a long or complex one, provides opportunities to reinforce the learner at relatively frequent intervals. But, if a task is practiced only in sections, the connections between the sections may not be practiced adequately. Many children practice musical compositions by parts, rarely practicing the entire composition as a unit. As a result, they may achieve a perfect performance of individual sections, but, because they have not practiced the transitions, they may be unable to bridge the gap from one unit to another.

Most studies have indicated that distributed practice is superior to massed practice, but this is not always the case. Distributed practice seems to offer little advantage over massed practice, for example, when people are learning novel and highly interesting tasks. This fact helps to explain the usual superiority of distributed practice when learners are not particularly well motivated. Almost inevitably we make errors in the course of practice, and these errors, if we repeat them, can become well established. The frequency of errors increases when we become inattentive due to fatigue and boredom. Distributed practice, since it provides opportunities for rest and a change of activity, tends to reduce errors resulting from inattention.

Distributed practice also provides an opportunity for selective forgetting of inappropriate responses. Errors often occur during practice, but the learner usually does not make errors as frequently as he makes correct responses. Consequently, during rest periods there is a tendency for these erroneous responses, since they are less frequently practiced, to drop out of his performance more readily than the more frequently practiced correct responses. Distributed practice may also help the learner detect those portions of the task that he has learned inadequately, since he will tend to forget them more readily than the well-established responses during rest periods.

When skills must be performed at a high rate of speed, we usually advise learners to practice first for accuracy and then for speed. This, in general, is good advice, provided the learner is later willing to sacrifice some of his accuracy temporarily in order to increase his rate of response. However, the nature of some tasks changes markedly when they are performed at a high rate of speed. As a result, practice at low rates of speed on some tasks may set up habits that must later be abandoned. Or the learner, practicing at a low rate of speed, may fail to acquire some of the responses necessary for performance at the higher rate. Firing a rifle accurately at a stationary target, for example, calls for some of the same responses required to hit a moving target. But some of the responses acquired through shooting at the stationary target may interfere with learning to hit moving objects, and the learner must extinguish these responses in addition to acquiring new ones; he cannot simply perform the same act at a higher rate of speed. Clearly, the instructor must analyze skill performances carefully. Even those that appear very similar may, on closer examination, present quite different problems to the learner.

Summary: The Importance of Skill Performance. Skills, unlike concepts, do not help us organize our perceptions or interpret our experiences, but they frequently have an indirect effect on the way we view our social and physical environments. Skills are obviously important for their instrumental value—that is, for their usefulness in helping us satisfy many of our needs. But we sometimes overlook their importance as indirect sources of satisfaction, or we fail to recognize their effects on our perceptions of ourselves. People who move about awkwardly, who are clumsy with tools and utensils, or who lack the agility and coordination essential in many games are usually treated differently from persons who are more skillful. Almost inevitably, they come to regard themselves as different and, perhaps, as inferior.

Adults, including teachers, often overlook the importance of skills in the lives of children and adolescents, perhaps because, as adults, we have already achieved some measure of skill in those activities that are important to us and take our competence for granted. And, as adults, we live in a world in which physical accomplishments are less important than social or intellectual achievements. We sometimes forget that achieving competence in a skill can enhance a child's feelings of personal worth, increase his sense of confidence, and affect his behavior in other areas well beyond that particular skill. Failure to acquire some skill, on the other hand, can produce a sense of defeat that pervades other aspects of the child's life. In a study of children's motor performances, for example, a positive relationship was found between measures of skill and measures of personal adjustment.[5]

---

5. Harold E. Jones, *Motor Performance and Growth* (Berkeley, Cal.: University of California Press, 1949), p. 152.

There is some degree of specificity in skills—that is, people tend to be superior in some skills and mediocre or poor in others. This means, of course, that, while most people are not likely to become skilled at everything they try, most of them are capable of developing a satisfying level of competence in one or more skills—provided, of course, that their potentials are assessed accurately and that they receive instruction based on their abilities and a careful analysis of the skills they are trying to learn.

PROBLEM SOLVING

How does problem solving differ from skill learning? Can we, for example, make a meaningful distinction between the performance of a tennis player as he competes with a clever opponent and the behavior of an expert chess player as he maneuvers his chessmen in a carefully planned attack? Both skill learning and problem solving are complex behaviors. In both, understanding the nature of the task is critically important if we are to become competent. Skilled performance often calls for judgment and strategy, while problem solving sometimes requires careful, precise movements and manipulations.

One rather obvious distinction is that in skill performance the final motor response is all important. This is the end toward which all previous cognitive activity and practice have been directed. In problem solving, however, manipulative behavior, if it does occur, is simply a means to an end. The student writing down an answer to an arithmetic problem is manipulating a pencil, but this is incidental to the fact that he is indicating the choice of a particular response. The person trying to fit a piece into a puzzle is, in effect, testing a hypothesis about that piece and its relationship to other parts of the puzzle. In both cases, the really important activity is cognitive rather than manipulative.

There is another difference between skills and problem-solving ability: problem solving does not reach the autonomous stage of a fully developed skill. Most of us can tie our shoes or wash dishes while thinking of other things, but we are not very successful at solving problems while giving our attention to other matters. Probably everyone has, on occasion, suddenly perceived the solution to a problem that he had set aside or dismissed as too difficult, but our successful problem-solving performances usually occur in full awareness of what we are trying to do.

These differences help us distinguish between skills and problem solving, but they do not clearly define problem-solving behavior itself. The cat trying to escape from a puzzle box, the student trying to solve a quadratic equation, the artist trying to create a certain effect, and the scientist trying to organize his knowledge of some phenomenon into a comprehensive theory are all trying to solve a problem. But it is apparent that both the tasks and the behaviors differ greatly.

Part of our difficulty in analyzing and describing problem-solving behavior results from our failure to define with any clarity what we mean by a "problem." It would perhaps help us in our thinking about problem solving if we distinguished between *problems that are presented or given* and *problems to be discovered or identified.* In some situations, the problem is known, or specified, and there is some standard procedure that, if followed, will result in a solution. Sometimes, however, the problem is undefined or unstructured, and there may be no established means of attacking it. "Convert 2.5 meters into inches" calls for quite different problem-solving behavior than does "Give some reasonable explanation for the fact that no mammals are green."

According to J. P. Guilford, problems like the first of these two arouse *convergent thinking* processes.[6] We think convergently when we arrive at answers through the use of known rules and information or when we engage in criticism and evaluation. Problems of the second type call for *divergent thinking*—that is, for thinking that is less determined by knowledge specifically related to the problem or by established rules and procedures; rather than trying to find a single "correct" answer, we may attempt to produce a variety of explanations or an unusual solution.

Educators frequently stress the need for greater emphasis on divergent thinking and the desirability of encouraging creativity in students. But, outside the arts—and sometimes even there—we often neglect or discourage divergent thinking. It is understandable, of course, that schools should emphasize conventional solutions to many of the problems we expect young people to face. As we noted in Chapter One, all cultures attempt to teach their members culturally acceptable solutions to problems, and convergent thinking does enable us to deal with many problems in

6. J. P. Guilford, "Three Faces of Intellect," *American Psychologist* (August 1959), pp. 469–79.

a satisfactory and efficient manner. But sometimes, in an effort to help and to encourage students, or simply in an attempt to speed the learning process, we fill in so many of the unknowns that a problem that should have called for divergent thinking arouses only convergent thought processes and very conventional responses.

What are the effects on problem-solving ability of stressing problems calling for convergent thinking? Emphasis on learning solutions to problems rather than discovering problems or seeking answers to problems may result in the learner's assuming that solutions exist for all problems and that, if he wishes to become an efficient problem solver, his task is to learn solutions. As Guilford has pointed out,[7] the ways in which we think about problems are determined, at least in part, by the nature of the problems themselves. But, of course, simply encountering a problem calling for divergent thought does not guarantee that we will think divergently if we have had little experience with such problems. Research [8] suggests that our performance on problems calling for originality and creativity can be improved by training and experience. This is encouraging, but it also suggests that such abilities may fail to develop if the proper opportunities never occur —if we fail to receive the necessary stimulation and experience.

Everyone agrees that teaching people to solve problems is an important objective of education. But, obviously, not everyone is in complete agreement as to just what is meant by "solving problems." Some teachers apparently believe that problem solving can be equated with the learning and retention of solutions to problems. For them, the well-trained student who can jot down the correct answers to multiplication problems with scarcely a pause is a highly efficient problem solver. Other teachers disagree; they see problem solving as a matter of learning how to think about problems, of developing modes of attack that are applicable to a wide array of problems.

The majority of teachers, however, straddle the fence on this issue. They teach solutions to many problems, particularly to those

---

7. Guilford, *loc. cit.*

8. I. Maltzman, *et al.*, "Experimental Studies in the Training of Originality," *Psychological Monographs,* No. 493 (1960), and S. Parnes and A. Meadow, "Effects of 'Brainstorming' Instructions on Creative Problem Solving by Trained and Untrained Subjects," *Journal of Educational Psychology* (August 1959), pp. 171–76.

problems they are reasonably sure their students will encounter repeatedly. They also attempt to teach certain principles that will have more general applicability. But we cannot be taught solutions to all the problems we will encounter during our lifetime, and we could not retain them if they could be taught to us. Nor would any particular learning set be completely applicable to all problems. So teachers compromise—they try to teach "useful" information as well as principles and generalizations they hope their students will be able to apply to a wide variety of problems. This is perhaps what educators have in mind when they speak of learning "basic skills" in arithmetic, reading, or some other subject—an unfortunate use of the term "skill."

Gagné has pointed out that problem solving, like concept formation, is a *nonreproductive* type of learning.[9] That is, the desired response or solution is not presented as part of the problem situation. In learning a skill or in verbal learning, for example, the performance or the words to be learned are part of the learning situation. This is not so in the case of problem solving, where the learner is required to make a response that has not been given directly to him.

Questions about the nature of problem solving may seem tedious and unnecessary, and they may provoke teachers to remark: "Look! *I* know a problem when I see one, and *I* know what *I* mean by problem solving." But obviously, while each teacher may know what *he* means by problems and problem solving, not all teachers mean the same thing. More important, if teachers differ on this point, they very likely differ on two other matters of major importance: how to evaluate problem solving and how to go about improving problem-solving performance.

If we consider problem solving to be a matter of learning solutions to problems, we can treat it as another form of instrumental learning. We can present stimuli (problems) and reinforce appropriate responses (solutions). Or we can assume that the problem solver probably makes a series of responses, each response serving as a stimulus for the next response until a successful solution is finally achieved.

A form of research on problem solving that Woodworth and

9. R. M. Gagné, "Problem Solving," in A. W. Melton, ed., *Categories of Human Learning* (New York: Academic Press, 1964), p. 311.

Schlosberg have labeled the *process-tracing experiment*[10] has been based on this view of problem solving. A subject is presented with a problem, and the experimenter seeks to answer the question "What does the subject do in achieving a solution?" Subjects are observed closely as they work. Often they are asked to introspect and attempt to report on their "hunches" and on the reasoning lying back of their overt responses. The sequence of responses leading to solutions is analyzed, and the responses of "good" problem solvers are compared with those of "poor" problem solvers.

This approach has failed to provide us with much useful information about the improvement of problem-solving ability for two reasons: first, because it is based upon the assumption that the immediate problem situation and the subject's responses to it are the principal determinants of problem-solving behavior; second, because it assumes that these observable events are the principal determinants of problem solving, an assumption that ignores the fact that performance in a problem-solving situation is determined to a great extent by previous experience and performance. Many psychologists have stressed the fact that the problem solver adds something to the situation when he solves a problem—that his successful solution is not dependent solely upon those stimuli presented by the problem itself. Bartlett has applied the expression "filling in the gaps,"[11] and Bruner speaks of the problem solver "going beyond the information given."[12]

What is this "something" that the successful problem solver adds to the problem situation? One answer is that he adds the effects of previous experience. Robert Gagné has pointed out that, as long as the learner is making responses that are "stimulus tied," that is, responses made directly and solely to the particular stimulus pattern confronting him—he is simply engaged in discrimination learning, not in problem solving. This view of problem solving has led Gagné to suggest that

> . . . the solving of a problem is a set of events which must have been *preceded* by learning. In order to solve anagrams, one must pre-

---

10. R. S. Woodworth and H. Schlosberg, *Experimental Psychology*, rev. ed. (New York: Holt, Rinehart and Winston, 1954), pp. 815–25.
11. F. C. Bartlett, *Thinking. An Experimental and Social Study* (New York: Basic Books, 1958).
12. J. S. Bruner, *et al.*, "Going Beyond the Information Given," in *Contemporary Approaches to Cognition* (Cambridge, Mass.: Harvard University Press, 1957).

> viously have learned words and their meanings; to solve water-jar problems, one must have learned to add and subtract numbers; to solve a pendulum problem, one must have learned about pendulums, and perhaps other things as well.[13]

Other psychologists have agreed with Gagné and have suggested two different ways of viewing problem solving: (1) as the operation of *learning sets* or (2) as *transfer of learning.*

Harlow's monkeys, as we have noted, became more and more adept at solving discrimination or oddity problems as they became more and more experienced with a number of different problems. They ceased to be "stimulus tied," and, instead of making their choice on the basis of some simple principle such as "Always choose the larger container," they eventually appeared to be operating on the basis of some higher-order principle applicable to a variety of problems. Such a principle might be "Shift your choice if the first choice is unsuccessful" or "Discover the relevant stimulus dimension; that is, determine whether one should respond to size, color, position, and so on."

Rudolph Schulz has offered another suggestion: [14] that problem solving is really a matter of transfer of learning. In fact, Schulz argues that there are no problems except in those situations where transfer from previous learning is incomplete or negative. Where there is insufficient transfer from previous experience, the individual does not know exactly how to respond. He has, in other words, encountered a problem. Where transfer is perfect, a person has no experience of being confronted with a problem; he simply makes the previously acquired response that the situation calls for. Note that, according to this view, the student who has thoroughly learned the multiplication tables is not really solving a problem when he responds to the question "How much is 17 × 3?"

Viewing problem solving as transfer of learning might be more helpful if we knew more about the nature of transfer. However, as Schulz points out:

> The present conception of problem solving as transfer has the important virtue of keeping research on problem solving, at worst, one step removed from possible application in matters of educational practice. That is, insofar as it is correct to assume that education is predominantly a problem in transfer of training, the task of translating

13. Gagné, *op. cit.*, p. 293.
14. R. W. Schulz, "Problem Solving Behavior and Transfer," *Harvard Educational Review* (Winter 1960), pp. 61–77.

laboratory findings in the technology of education should be facilitated by the present conception of problem solving.[15]

These views of problem solving, either as transfer or as set, are obviously not incompatible with each other. Some individuals, of course, may ask, "But which is the *right* way to think about problem solving?" As Howard Kendler has observed:

> . . . the selection of any theoretical model . . . is in the last analysis a decision having *no truth character*. That is, in spite of the fact that the choice of a model may, and usually does, influence both experimentation and theorizing, the choice itself cannot be evaluated as being right or wrong. . . . the most we can do is to attempt, in a sincere and conscientious manner, to understand the implications of such decisions . . . .[16]

We can regard a problem as a situation for which the individual's previous experience has not provided him with a ready response. And it probably makes little difference which model (transfer or set) guides our thinking about his behavior in such circumstances. Both are useful ways of thinking about problem solving and whether we adopt one viewpoint or the other, the tasks of both learner and teacher remain essentially the same. The necessary experiences must be decided upon, acquired, and, perhaps, organized into some readily transferable principle. Through cues and directions, the teacher can attempt to increase the probability that the experiences will transfer or that the relevance of principles will be perceived by the problem solver.

Variables Affecting Problem-Solving Performance. Different learners show wide variations in their ability to solve similar problems, and the same learner may be much more successful in dealing with some problems than with others. How can we account for these differences in performance, and what can be done to improve problem-solving performance?

Gagné has suggested that the independent variables in any problem-solving situation can be considered under two general headings: (1) conditions within the learner and (2) conditions in the problem situation.[17] Conditions within the learner include

---

15. *Ibid.*
16. Howard H. Kendler, "'What Is Learned?' A Theoretical Blind Alley," *Psychological Review* (July 1952), pp. 269–77.
17. Robert M. Gagné, *The Conditions of Learning* (New York: Holt, Rinehart and Winston, 1965), pp. 162–64.

such factors as motivation, intelligence, the effects of previous experience, and the presence or absence of a problem-solving set. Conditions in the problem situation include the organization of the problem, the manner in which it is presented, and the directions given to the problem solver.

Conditions within the learner. Not every experience or every set necessarily facilitates problem solving. Luchins found [18] that when individuals learned a certain procedure for measuring quantities of water by using two jars, they persisted in using this method on later problems where it was no longer efficient. Birch and Rabinowitz presented college students with a task calling for them to construct a pendulum, using either a switch or a relay as a weight.[19] With few exceptions, students who had previously used relays in a wiring problem selected the switch as a weight; those who had used switches in their wiring problem, used relays in the pendulum problem. Both groups explained their choices by remarks such as "Anyone can see this one is better as a pendulum weight." Apparently, having had experience with either switches or relays in one situation, the students had difficulty perceiving their potential usefulness in another type of problem.

But if problem solving is "a set of events which must have been preceded by learning," experience is an obvious necessity for successful problem solving. However, it must be relevant experience. Our discussions of transfer and of learning sets suggest that experiences that are organized into a hierarchical pattern of learning or into principles are most likely to lead to improved problem solving.

Some educators have suggested that students' ability to solve problems would be most improved if their experiences resulted in their learning "strategies" or "styles" of thinking; that we should teach students "how to think." It is probably possible to teach problem-solving strategies, and quite possibly we should place more stress on this type of experience. It is doubtful, however, whether such practice, to the exclusion of other experiences, would necessarily produce superior problem solvers. Efficient problem solving seems to call for both "content" principles and heuristic prin-

---

18. A. S. Luchins, "Mechanization in Problem Solving: The Effect of *'Einstellung,'*" *Psychological Monographs,* No. 248 (1942).
19. H. G. Birch and H. S. Rabinowitz, "The Negative Effect of Previous Experience on Productive Thinking," *Journal of Experimental Psychology* (February 1951), pp. 121–25.

ciples—that is, we need to have acquired a broad body of well-organized knowledge, as well as some problem-solving strategies. This is the function of experience in problem solving: to provide opportunities to learn how to attack problems and to permit the acquisition of a fund of potentially transferable responses.

Conditions in the problem situation. We have discussed the probability that effective problem solving requires the transfer of previous learning to a new situation or calls for the problem solver to derive higher-order principles from simpler principles that he has already learned. This suggests that an important variable in problem solving is the manner in which the problem is structured. We can, of course, attempt to determine whether the learner has already acquired the necessary prerequisite responses and attempt to build upon his prior experiences in a hierarchical fashion.

As Bruner has pointed out,[20] success in problem solving is more likely if, in representing the problem, we use symbolic propositions, procedures, or images that are already familiar to the problem solver. It is probably also helpful if we can organize the task so that he has to recall a minimum number of separate principles or items of information, since, as Gagné has noted, "The component principles . . . must in some sense be 'held in mind' all at once, or be reactivated at will in close time succession in problem solving." [21]

The effects of problem presentation on problem solution are illustrated by a relatively simple task devised by Judson and Cofer.[22] Subjects were presented with groups of words and asked to indicate the one word that was not related to the other three. When the words "subtract," "increase," "multiply," and "add" were presented in that order, "increase" was most frequently rejected, whereas the order "multiply," "increase," "add," "subtract" led to "subtract" being rejected. The effects of previous experience were also evident in subjects' responses to series such as "prayer," "temple," "cathedral," "skyscraper." Subjects with strong religious backgrounds were more likely to reject "skyscraper," while other subjects selected "prayer" as the unrelated word.

---

20. See Chapter One, p. 10.
21. Gagné, *The Conditions of Learning, op. cit.,* p. 162.
22. A. J. Judson and C. N. Cofer, "Reasoning as an Associative Process: I. 'Direction' in a Simple Verbal Problem," *Psychological Report* (December 1956), pp. 469–76.

FIGURE 14
NINE-DOT PROBLEM

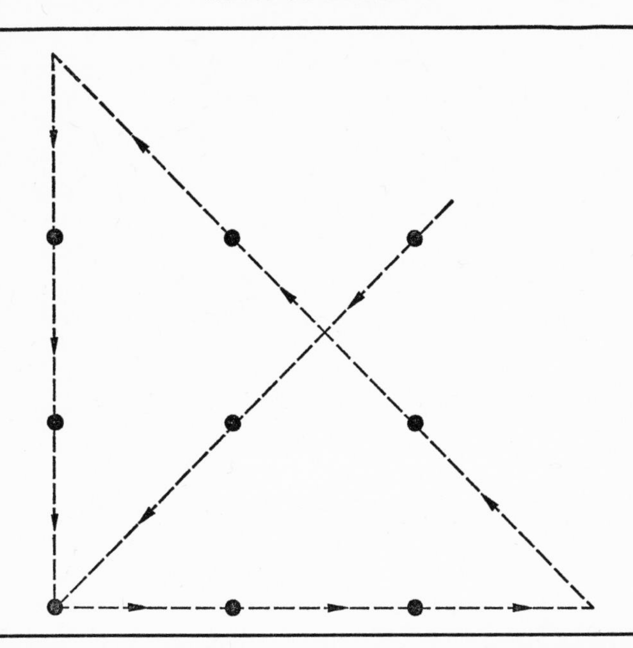

Instructions can be regarded both as a part of the problem and as an important variable affecting problem-solving behavior. Gagné has suggested that directions serve both a *constraining* function and a *contributing* function.[23]

Directions can be used by the teacher to define the problem —to inform the learner of the goal toward which he is working and of the general nature of the solution he is seeking. Viewed this way, directions may be thought of as constraining the problem solver. They may indicate the type of acceptable response he will make, "channel" his thinking along certain lines, and keep him within the possible range of correct responses. Provided such "channeling" is done intelligently and stops short of actually providing the solution, it can facilitate problem solving by increasing the probability that relevant responses will be made. For example, the nine-dot problem shown in Figure 14 calls for connecting all dots

23. Robert M. Gagné, "Problem Solving," in A. W. Melton, ed., *Categories of Human Learning* (New York: Academic Press, 1964), pp. 303–08.

with no more than four straight lines. The percentage of correct responses is increased if learners are told that the problem situation does not require them to stay within the square formed by the dots.

Directions can also serve a *contributing* function by stimulating the problem solver's recall of relevant principles or subordinate capabilities that he has already acquired. If we choose to regard problem solving as transfer, directions may be viewed as a means of facilitating transfer of previous learning.

Directions may also be used to identify the more important parts of the problem situation. If we are to solve problems correctly and efficiently, we must respond appropriately to the different elements in the problem. This means, of course, that we must be able to differentiate among these elements and, in some cases, ignore some of them and concentrate on others.

Sometimes subtle differences in directions can lead to improved problem solving. Judson and Cofer, for example, found that subjects were more likely to solve a problem calling for them to swing one string within reach of another by attaching a weight to one end if they had previously learned a list of words in which "rope" was associated with "swing." [24] On the other hand, if "rope" had been associated with "hemp," the problem solution was less likely to occur.

Many of the problems we encounter have, of course, no formal or clearly specified directions, and we must rely upon our ability to identify similar problem situations and recall previously appropriate responses. This suggests the desirability of learning some general directions to guide our problem-solving activity. Bloom and Broder have suggested that students might learn a governing set to help them break harmful or handicapping sets.[25] Students, for example, often expect immediate success and assume that mistakes indicate stupidity. Or they adopt a "speed set,"—that is, they mistakenly assume that all problems must be solved in the shortest possible time. Their ability to solve problems might be improved if they are taught to ask themselves, "Did I learn something from that mistake? What did I learn? Am I making certain as-

---

24. Judson and Cofer, *op. cit.*
25. B. S. Bloom and L. J. Broder, *Problem-solving Processes of College Students: An Exploratory Investigation* (Chicago: University of Chicago Press, 1950).

sumptions? Should some of my assumptions about this problem be questioned? Is there a different way of looking at this situation?"

Evaluating problem solving. Many problem-solving sets and student attitudes about problem solving result from the ways in which we evaluate problem-solving performance. Our evaluation procedures derive, in turn, from our views about the nature of problem solving.

If we regard problem solving as simply another form of instrumental learning, it is appropriate to evaluate problem-solving performance on the basis of (1) *rate of attainment* and (2) *degree of correctness of the performance.* Rate of attainment, or the speed with which a person arrives at a solution to a problem, can be measured by determining the amount of time before a correct solution is reached, the number of presentations of a particular type of problem before success is achieved, or the number and kind of errors made. Teachers are usually aware of variations among students in the speed with which they learn to solve problems, but most teachers' judgments of rate of attainment are very subjective. It would be quite unusual to find a teacher actually timing learners or counting the number of presentations before a problem is solved. On the other hand, teachers frequently encourage students to solve problems as rapidly as possible and evaluate problem-solving performance on the basis of the number of correct responses made within a given time limit.

Critics of these conventional evaluation techniques have pointed out that such procedures presuppose that problem solving occurs on an all-or-none basis: the learner either solves the problem or he does not. These critics point out that some learners, although they fail to solve the problem, come closer to the solution than do others and that some errors are "intelligent" errors, while others are "stupid" or nonsensical. Evaluating problem solving on the basis of right or wrong answers, they argue, tells us little about how a learner goes about solving a problem and, therefore, provides us with little or no basis for correcting or assisting him.

We have noted Gagné's point that problem solving differs from other forms of learning in that it does not call for the learner to acquire a specific response that is presented to him as part of the learning situation. If problem solving is "nonreproductive" in this sense, we are really assuming that the problem solver's response is not merely applicable to a single specific problem but is *generalizable to an entire class of problems of this type.* As Gagné has noted:

> No one would be particularly excited to learn that a monkey had solved a single oddity problem. Rather, it is the fact that the monkey solves a variety of problems with a number of different stimulus objects, resembling each other only insofar as they can be classified as "oddity problems" by the experimenter, which makes it possible to infer problem solving (or learning set). . . . Accordingly, the demonstration of generalizability may be considered a good differential criterion for the distinguishing of problem solving from other varieties of learning.[26]

Not only may *generalizability of solution* within a class of problems be a good criterion for distinguishing problem solving from other forms of learning, it may also be a good basis for judging how well an individual has learned to solve problems. If a learner can make an appropriate response to only one problem within a class of related problems there is reason to question whether he has really learned to solve a problem or whether he has merely learned a simple association between a stimulus and a response.

Problem Solving in Groups. Many educators have stressed the values of learning to solve problems as a member of a group and have implied that group problem solving is more desirable and more efficient than individual problem solving. Unfortunately, the objectives of group problem solving have never been very clearly defined. There are very good reasons for having children learn to work together, and solving problems in groups is one way of achieving this goal. But such a desirable outcome has little or nothing to do with the questions of whether or not groups solve problems more efficiently than do individuals working alone.

The questions that need to be answered about group versus individual problem solving are: Is the group more effective in achieving solutions than the same individuals working separately? Does the performance of the group exceed the performance of the ablest individual in the group? Does working in a group inhibit some individuals? Do groups solve problems differently from individuals working alone?

---

26. Gagné, "Problem Solving," *op. cit.*, p. 300.

The answers to these questions seem to depend on such factors as the nature of the problem, the type of leadership provided for the group, the way in which labor is divided within the group, communication among group members, and whether group members are motivated to achieve group goals or their own individual goals.

If the group is working on a problem that can be broken down into parts, the group probably has an advantage over an equal number of individuals working alone, provided the group is organized so that those working on portions of the task receive sufficient information from one another to coordinate their efforts. A group may possess jointly more information than any single individual. But this is an advantage only if this information can be communicated to all members of the group and if the group acts on this information. Skillful group leadership calls for providing an opportunity for all members to contribute. In large groups this process of communication may be cumbersome, but this disadvantage may be offset by some improvement in accuracy, since each member's work is subject to scrutiny by the group. There is also some evidence that the frustrations inherent in problem solving may be reduced by working in groups and that students working in groups are more persistent than those working alone.

But it is probably a mistake to assume that designating several individuals as a group will necessarily arouse group problem-solving behavior. If there is no intragroup communication, if the abler members of the group go unheard or are dominated by the less able members, or if individual members are unconcerned about group goals, there is probably little or no advantage in group problem solving. The fact of the matter is that we know even less about group problem solving than we do about problem solving by individuals, and claimed advantages for problem solving in groups should be examined critically.

Whether we are studying the problem-solving behavior of individuals or of groups, we find it as baffling and frustrating as it is intriguing. Every aspect of human learning that we have considered up to this point—conditioning, motivation, verbal behavior, concept formation, retention, and transfer—bears some relationship to problem solving. Teachers are often frustrated both by its complexity and by the fact that their role in facilitating problem solving is an ambiguous one. In most learning situations, the teacher need feel no hesitancy in giving all the assistance he can. In teaching children to spell or to grasp the meaning of a definition, the teacher can take a direct, active role. But in problem solving, even though he knows the solution or the means of solving the problem, the teacher must often stand back and allow the learner to struggle. When he does try to help, the teacher often finds it difficult to draw the line between arranging a too-easy success for the learner and allowing him to become discouraged.

Despite the difficulties it presents, human problem solving is a fascinating subject. Man's ability to adapt to varied and unusual circumstances is impressive. He clearly excels all other forms of life in his ability to cope with a wide variety of physical and social environments. Not a very impressive animal physically, he has compensated so effectively for his physical inadequacies that he now is able to move through and above the earth's atmosphere at tremendous speeds, travel beneath the surface of the sea, and multiply his strength enormously by mechanical and chemical means. By use of the computers and calculators that he has developed, he is even able to transcend some of his intellectual limitations.

But man has been far less successful in solving his social and political problems, and the progress of the behavioral sciences in this area has been painfully slow. As Dael Wolfle has observed, "It is much more difficult to capture the essence of such [social] problems in the laboratory or under controlled conditions than it is to capture the essence of a physical or biological problem." [27] Yet it is in finding solutions to social problems that we may very well be engaged in a race with disaster. Although we hardly have grounds for optimism, two bright spots are apparent: the study of human problem solving is receiving increasing attention; and man's overall record as a problem solver has been truly remarkable.

Suggestions for Class Discussion and Further Investigation

1. The handwriting of most of us, as adults, is less legible than it was during our school years, and those of us who write the most frequently have the least legible handwriting.

---

27. Dael Wolfle, "Social Problems and Social Science," *Science* (March 11, 1966), p. 1177.

How do you account for the fact that greater practice, in this case, does not seem to result in greater skill?

2. Do you think that the desirable length of practice sessions may also be a function of the characteristics of the learner as well as the characteristics of the task?
3. Consider some skill in which you are reasonably proficient. How would you go about preparing to teach this skill to others? How would you actually teach the skill?
4. Our schools have been criticized for emphasizing drill and the learning of facts in the elementary grades and deferring problem solving and reflective thinking until the secondary-school years. If this criticism is valid, what are the consequences of this practice?
5. Persons who agree that computers cannot really "think" often point out that the computer can do only what it is programed to do. If the program, consisting of a set of directions to the computer, represents the experience of the person who constructs it, what is the difference between programing a computer to solve problems and teaching a student to solve problems?
6. Many of our most distinguished scientists have devoted their lives to studying problems that the majority of people overlooked or ignored. How can we develop in students an awareness of problems?

Suggestions for Further Reading

Although it also deals with the topics of motives, attitudes, and values of teen-agers in a representative group of high schools, Jane S. Coleman, *The Adolescent Society* (New York: The Free Press of Glencoe, 1961), points out the pervasive importance of skills, particularly athletic skills, in the world of the adolescent.

Some of the most intensive study of skill learning has been carried out by industrial psychologists and by psychologists interested in the applications of theories of skill learning to training. Two articles that approach skill learning from this position are: Paul M. Fitts, "Skill Training," in R. Glaser, ed., *Training Research and Education* (Pittsburgh, Pa.: University of Pittsburgh Press, 1962); and F. V. Taylor, "Psychology and the Design of Machines," *American Psychologist,* Vol. XII (1957), pp. 245–58.

A broader discussion of the learning of skills is contained in E. A. Bilodeau and I. McD. Bilodeau, "Motor Skills Learning," *Annual Review of Psychology,* Vol. XII (1961), pp. 243–80.

It has become popular to state that we can teach anything to children of any age if we set about it in the right manner. Jean Piaget, in two books, *Judgment and Reasoning in the Child* and *Language and Thought of the Child* (Paterson, N.J.: Littlefield, Adams, 1959), has suggested that the ability to solve problems may be at least partly determined by the learner's stage of development. A more concise discussion of Piaget's more recent views is contained in an article by D. E. Berlyne, "Recent Developments in Piaget's Work," *British Journal of Educational Psychology,* Vol. XXVII (1957), pp. 1–12.

The development of computers has led a number of psychologists to consider the possibility of their use in testing theoretical models of human problem solving. Two particularly well-written articles on this topic are Carl Hovland's "Computer Simulation of Thinking," *American Psychologist,* Vol. XV (1960), pp. 687–93; and A. Newell, J. C. Shaw, and H. A. Simon, "Elements of a Theory of Human Problem-Solving," *Psychological Review,* Vol. LXV (1958), pp. 151–66.

The role of language in problem solving has been examined by Howard H. Kendler and Tracy S. Kendler in "Vertical and Horizontal Processes in Problem-Solving," *Psychological Review,* Vol. LXIX (1962), pp. 1–16.

Index

Page number followed by *n.* indicates footnote; page number in italics indicates illustration.

Abstraction, 84, 136, 148. *See also* Concept formation
Adolescent Society, The, 64
Allport, Gordon, 145
Amsel, A., 56, 57
Anxiety reduction, 67–71, 80–81. *See also* Drive reduction; Punishment
Ausubel, D. P., 143
Automation, 149, 150

Baker, K. E., 136
Bartlett, F. C., 162
Bates, Marston, 5
Behavior: consummatory, 73, 75, 77; control of, 6, 14, 29, 41, 51, 55, 71, 72, 73, 76, 85, 86; extinction of, *see* Extinction; terminal, 142–43; transposition, 99–101, *100*. *See also* Instrumental behavior; Respondent behavior; Verbal behavior
Behavior change, 3–4, 24–25, 29–31, 33, 40, 42, 50, 51, 76, 80, 109, 110, 147–48. *See also* Conditioning; Reinforcement
Behavior events, 4, 5, 6, 44
Birch, H. G., 165
Blair, Glenn M., 16
Bloom, B. S., 168
Book, William F., 152*n.*
Broder, L. J., 168
Brown, E. L., 151*n.*
Brown, Roger, 92
Bruner, Jerome S., 10, 11, 16, 17, 162, 166
Bugelski, B. R., 47, 66, 67, 70, 131, 132
Buxton, C. D., 32

Cadwallader, T. C., 131, 132
Carmichael, L., 118, 119*n.*
Cell assemblies, 69
Chevalier, J. A., 68*n.*
Child, I. L., 57
Classical conditioning, 26–29, 34, 36, 41, 68–69, 79, 90–91, *90*
Cofer, C. N., 166, 168
Cognitive dissonance, 78–80
Coleman, James S., 13, 64
Concept formation, 29, 41, 84, 93–106, *97, 98,* 128, 134, 147, 167, 171. *See also* Generalization; Learning sets
Concepts. *See* Concept formation
Conditioned inhibition, 37, 38
Conditioning, 37–38, 53, 73, 77, 79, *88,* 91, 110, 171. *See also* Classical conditioning; Instrumental conditioning; Reinforcement
Consonance, 79, 80
Consummatory behavior, 73, 75, 77
Continuity theory, 103
Coordination, 149, 150, 152

Dallenbach, K. M., 112, 115
Davis, Robert A., 18
DeCecco, John P., 89
decision making, 41, 148, 164
Deese, James, 65, 131
Demonstration, 153–54
Discontinuity theory, 103
Discrete reflexes, 74
Discrimination, 52, 94, 103, 105, 133–35, 141, 142, 153, 163; variables affecting, 135–39
Discriminative control, 75

Disinhibition, 39
Dissonance, 69, 78, 79
Douvan, E., 57*n.*
Drive reduction, 48–54, 58–61, 70, 80. *See also* Anxiety reduction
Drives. *See* Drive reduction; Needs
Durkin, K., 57*n.*

Education: goals of, 3–5. *See also* Teacher; Teaching
Effective power, 10, 11
Emotion, 4, 43, 67–71, 86. *See also* Anxiety reduction
Environment, 14, 17, 19, 26, 28, 51, 54, 66, 73, 78, 79, 84, 85, 87, 93, 106, 126, 140–41, 157, 172
Error rate, 155–56, 169
Estes, W. K., 73
Experience (learning), 15, 16, 24, 25, 42, 63, 86, 94, 104–06, 114, 127, 128, 134, 140, 141, 160, 162–66
Extinction, 28, 33, 35–40, 56, 72, 74, 77, 78, 80, 99, 100, 101, 109, 111, 154, 157

Feedback, 12, 30, 32, 33, 150, 153, 155
Festinger, L., 78, 79
Fitts, Paul M., 150
Fitzgerald, D., 143*n.*
Flexman, R. E., 151*n.*
Forgetting, 111–14, 115, 117, 124, 156; interference theory of, 112–14, 115, 121; trace theory of, 111. *See also* Retention
Frustration, 40, 56–57. *See also* Anxiety reduction

Gage, N. L., 15
Gagné, Robert M., 136, 141–44, 161, 162, 163, 164, 166, 167, 169, 170
Generalization, 94, 99, 100, 101, 118–20, 133–35, 140, 141, 142–45, 161, 170; variables affecting, 135–39. *See also* Learning sets; Principles
Gerard, R. W., 139, 140
Gilliland, A. R., 115*n.*
Goss, A. E., 96, 98*n.*
Guilford, J. P., 159, 160

Hanfmann, Eugenia, 97*n.*
Hardman, G. W., Jr., 131
Harlow, Harry F., 48–49, 134, 139, 163
Hebb, D. O., 60, 68, 69, 70*n.*
Highet, Gilbert, 6, 7*n.*
Hilgard, E., 10*n.*, 15*n.*, 19, 20*n.*
Hogan, H. P., 118, 119*n.*
Holmes, Frances B., 68*n.*
Homeostasis, 50–51, 54, 58–60
Hull, Clark L., 37, 38, 97*n.*
Hunt, J. McV., 127

Impulse control, 75
Information, 11, 30, 31, 116, 119, 120, 123, 150, 151, 154, 161, 162, 166, 171; acquisition of, 4, 11, 116; amount of, 10, 11; bits and chunks of, 116–18, *117*. *See also* Generalization; Retention
Inhibition, 37, 38, 112–13, 114
Initial Teaching Alphabet, 127
Instinctual behavior, 74
Instrumental behavior, 28–29, 36, 43, 44; language as form of, 86–89; and punishment, 73–76
Instrumental conditioning, 28, 29, 35, 69, 161, 169
Intelligence tests, 9, 138, 139, 148

James, William, 93, 150
Jenkins, J. G., 112, 115
Jersild, A. T., 68*n.*
Judgment, 148, 158
Judson, A. J., 166, 168

Kasanin, Jacob, 97*n.*
Katona, G., 118
Kelly, George A., 47
Kendler, Howard H., 101, 102*n.*, 103, 164
Kendler, Tracey S., 101, 102*n.*, 103
Kennedy, W. A., 57*n.*
Knowledge, 10, 11, 17, 64, 145, 148, 159, 166
Korchin, S. J., 68*n.*
Kreuger, W. C. F., 121*n.*, 122*n.*

Language, 84–106. *See also* Response, verbal; Verbal behavior
Learning: active avoidance, 72, 73; deductive, 105; experience, *see* Experience; hierarchical pattern of, 165, 166; inductive, 105; labeling of, 118, *119;* nonreproductive, 161, 169; operant, *see* Operant learning; passive avoidance of, 72, 73, 75; rate of, 33, 56; recoding of, 116, 118; reor-

ganization of, 115–20, 123; retrieval of, 109; storage of, 109. *See also* Task, learning of; Skill, learning of
Learning capacity, 4, 7, 11, 14, 138–39, 144
Learning intent, 123–24
Learning process, 8–17, 19, 26, 160
Learning retention. *See* Retention
Learning sets, 128, 129, 139, 143, 160–61, 163–65, 170. *See also* Concept formation; Generalization; Principles
Learning theory, 15–21, 42
Levine, S., 68*n.*
Linton, Ralph, 3
Lorge, Irving, 89
Luchins, A. S., 165

Maltzman, I., 160*n.*
Mand, 87–89, *88,* 91
Masserman, J. H., 73*n.*, 75
Matheny, W. G., 151*n.*
Meadow, A., 160*n.*
Meaning: connotative, 91, 104; denotative, 91, 104; situational, 91; of word, acquisition of, 87–92, *90*
Melton, A. W., 167*n.*
Melzak, R., 51–52
Miller, George A., 116
Milner, P., 60*n.*
Mode of representation, 10, 11
Motivation, 9, 104, 105, 112, 164, 171; and drive reduction, 50–54, 58–61, 67–71; and performance, 64–67, 152, 153, 156; as problem of teachers, 63–64, 81; and punishment, 64, 67, 71–78; and reinforcement, 30, 40, 41, 54–58, 58–61, 92; social 78–81; stimulus approach to, 54–58, 58–61, 64–65; and transfer, 127–28; views of, 47–50, 60–61
Moore, O. K., 127
Mowrer, O. H., 18, 86, 89

Needs, 12, 13, 48–54, 58–61, 63, 67, 78, 80
Newman, E. B., 115
Nine-dot problem, 167–68, *167*
Non-examples, 105–06

Olds, J., 60*n.*
Operant conditioning, *88,* 91
Operant learning, 78, 79, 89, 90
Osgood, C. E., 98, 99*n.*, 101, 129–31

Overlearning, 121–23, *122,* 137, 141–42, 152

Parnes, S., 160*n.*
Perception, 4, 18, 85, 93, 157
Performance, 12, 31–34, 37–38, 48, 56, 57, 64–67, 71, 103, 121, 126, 127, 132*n.*, 138–40, 151–59, 161, 162, 169, 170
Pollack, I., 117*n.*
Practice, 11–12, 123, 152, 154–57
Predifferentiation, 135–37
Principles, 102, 103, 106, 118, 119–20, 137, 140, 142, 151, 161, 165–66. *See also* Generalization; Learning sets
Proactive inhibition, 113, 114
Proactive transfer, 132, *132*
Problem solving, 10, 11, 29, 41, 71, 84, 85–86, 128, 136, 139, 147, 148, 158–72; group, 170–72
Problem-solving set, 165, 168, 169
Programed instruction, 12, 13, 142
Proprioceptive stimulus. *See* Stimulus
Punishment, 28, 29, 34, 35, 64, 67, 71–78

Rabinowitz, H. S., 165
Reactive inhibition, 37, 38
Recall, 110–11, 119, *119,* 123, 144
Recognition, 110, 111
Reflexes, 74, 149
Reinforcement, 12, 13, 14, 28, 29–35, 41, 43, 44, 52–58, 60, 65, 69, 73, 76, 77, 80, 81, 85, 92, 99, 100, 101, 103, 105, 111, 135, 154, 156, 161; and extinction, 35–40; fixed-interval, 55–56; fixed-ratio, 55; negative, 30; positive, 74, 87; primary, 34, 35; quality of, 55, 56–57; secondary, 34–35, 41, 50, 51, 53, 78, 80. *See also* Conditioning; Feedback
Reinforcement schedules, 33, 50, 55–56
Relearning, 110–11, 123–24, 126
Respondent behavior, 25–27, 28, 43, 44
Response: avoidance, *see* Learning, active avoidance, passive avoidance; conditioned, *see* Conditioning; discriminative, 103; echoic, 87–88, *88;* extinction of, *see* Behavior, extinction of; instrumental, 28–29, 33, 36; involuntary, 26, 28, 36; learned, 24; meaning, 90–91, *90;* movement, 149, 152; nonreversal, 101, *102;* operant, 73, 87; psychomotor, 89, 135, 141,

158; rate of, 56; reversal, 101–02, *102;* unconditioned, 27, 29, 90; unlearned, 24; verbal, 85, 86, 87–88, *88,* 89, 90, 92, 140. *See also* Behavior change; Classical conditioning; Learning; Reinforcement; Skills; Stimulus; Transfer
Response change. *See* Behavior change
Response substitution, 24, 25, 28
Response unit, 40
Retention, 15, 41, 105, 109–24, 128, 142–43, 160, 171. *See also* Forgetting
Retroactive inhibition, 112–13
Reward, 30, 35, 48, 57, 58, 64, 74, 77
Reynolds, B., 31*n.*
Roussel, J., 56, 57

Schlosberg, H., 162
Schulz, Rudolph W., 163
Scott, T. H., 51–52
Sensation, 4, 18, 85
Sets. *See* Learning sets
Shuford, E. H., Jr., 56–57
Skill, 12, 41, 59, 145, 147–49, 149–51, 159, 161; acquisition of, 4, 149, 151–57; autonomous phase of, 151, 152–53, 158; cognitive phase of, 151–54; fixation phase of, 151–54; importance of, 157–58; language, 84; nonverbal, 84; and practice, 152, 154–57; psychomotor, 12, 135, 136, 147, 148; teaching of, 151, 152, 153–57
Skinner, B. F., 12*n.*, 14, 34, 47, 64, 87, 93
Skinner box, 30, 36
Solomon, R. L., 72, 73, 75, 77
Spence, K. W., 99, 100, 101
Spontaneous recovery, 37–40
Staats, Arthur W., 27
Staats, Carolyn K., 27
Steps in research on learning, 19, *20*
Stimulus, 4, 10, 24, 26, 27, 28, 34, 35, 37–40, 47, 52–54, 54–58, 59, 65, 66, 67, 69, 73, 80, 81, 85, 87–91, *90,* 94, 99, 100–01, 102, 103, 105, 106, 118, 119*n.*, 123, 129, 130, 131, 136, 137, 138, 140, 150, 160, 161, 163, 170; competing, 66; conditioned, 26–27, 68, 90; discriminant, 87; distracting, 7, 39; external, 48, 50, 54, 64, 66, 86, 150, 153, 154; internal, 48, 66, 86, 150; levels of, 60; negative, 60, 66, 72; perceptual, 150, 153; positive, 53, 60, 61, 66; proprioceptive, 149, 150, 153, 154, 155; reinforcing, 12, 13, 50; unconditioned, 27, 29, 90, 91; verbal, 90, 92, 140
Stimulus event, 29–30, 94, 103, 134
Stimulus generalization. *See* Concept formation; Generalization
Stimulus pattern, 14, 91, 120–21, 133, 136
Stimulus satiation, 38–39, 50
Stimulus set, 24, 96, 97, 99
Stimulus substitution, 24, 25, 28
Strategy, 148, 151, 158, 165, 166
Symbol, 11, 50, 85, 86, 140, 166

Tact, 87, *88,* 89, 91
Task: affective, 9; concept-formation, 95–98, 164, 165, 166, 171; cognitive, 9, 148, 150, 158; learning of, 9, 10, 11, 29, 30, 32, 52, 64, 66, 71, 81, 93, 105, 113, 127, 129, 130*n.*, 136, 137–38, 139, 140, 144, 147, 148, 154–55, 156, 158, 159, 160; psychomotor, 9, 133, 136, 137, 151, 157; transfer, 128, 129, 130*n.*, 132*n.*, 137–38, 139, 142; verbal, 133, 136
Task element, 129, 138
Teacher, 8–21, 25–26, 38, 39, 41–42, 44, 55, 63–67, 70, 71, 72, 79, 80, 81, 95, 103–06, 109, 111, 119–21, 123, 126, 128, 135, 136, 138, 141–45, 148, 151, 153–54, 155, 157, 159–61, 167, 169, 170, 171; as motivator, 47, 49, 58, 81
Teaching, 3, 11, 15–17, 18, 19, 29, 36, 41–44, 103–06, 121, 126, 127, 135, 137, 140, 141–45, 147, 148, 151, 153–54, 160, 161
Teaching techniques, 42, 63, 81, 152
Terminal behavior, 142–43
Terrell, G., 57*n.*
Thinking, 85, 86; convergent, 159, 160; divergent, 159, 160. *See also* Response, verbal
Thorndike, E. L., 129, 144
Transfer: lateral, 143–44; of learning, 14, 15, 41, 126–45, 163–64, 165, 166, 168, 171; mental-discipline theory of, 128–29; negative, 127, 130–31, *130,* 133, 134, 137, 141, 163; positive, 129–31, *130,* 133, 134, 135, 136, 137, 138, 140, 141; proactive, 132, *132;* retroactive, 132, *132;* vertical, 143–44

Transfer elements, 129, 139, 140, 141
Transfer surface, 129–31, *130*, 132
Travers, R. M. W., 95*n.*
Tyler, R., 118, 119

Ullmer, Gilbert, 140*n.*
Underwood, B. J., 113, 114*n.*, 122
University of Illinois Aviation Psychology Laboratory, 151

Variables: behavior, 7; extinction, 37; of learning, 8, 15, 17, 29, 37, 42, 81, 85–89, 102, 131, 147; manipulation of, 14, 15; personality, 57; practice, 11–12; presentation, 10–11; problem-solving, 164–69; punishment, 74; reinforcement, 12–14, 50, 54, 55, 58; retention, 110, 111, 115–24, 128; transfer, 127, 128, 132, 135–39
Verbal behavior, 41, 84–106, 128, 135–36, 137, 140, 147, 151, 154, 161, 171

Walter, A. A., 118*n.*, 119*n.*
Waterhouse, I. K., 57
Whitehead, A. N., 21
Whiting, John, 88
Wiesley, M., 57*n.*
Wolfle, Dael, 172
Woodworth, R. S., 161

Young, P. T., 56–57

Zeaman, D., 31*n.*

1
F 2
G 3
H 4
I 5
J 6